Message to My Maidservants

From His Mouth to Our Ears

DESIRI OKOBIA

Copyright © 2021 Desiri Okobia

All rights reserved solely by the author. The author guarantees all contents are original and do not infringe upon the rights of any other person or work. No part of this book may be reproduced or transmitted in any form or by any means without prior written permission of the author.

Unless otherwise indicated:

Unless otherwise stated, Scripture quotations are taken from The Holy Bible, New King James Version. Public domain.

Scripture quotations marked NIV are taken from The Holy Bible, New International Version. Copyright © 1973, 1978, 1984 by Biblica, Inc.™ Used by permission. All rights reserved worldwide.

ISBN: 978-1-68536-201-0

This Edition Published by D.O.V Publishing House

Message to My Maidservants

From His Mouth to Our Ears

Message to My Maidservants consists of twelve powerful, faith-driven messages written for God. For the women that serve Him.

It covers many topics:

- ❖ Her Fears
- ❖ Her Purpose
- ❖ Her Gifts and Calling
- ❖ Her Heart Posture
- ❖ Her Future
- ❖ Her Father's Heart for Her

Dedication:

To the woman that God made.

Acknowledgements:

I would like to acknowledge the four amazing women who contributed their testimonies to making this book possible. Norma Rubi; Angela James; Cheryl Nembhard, Pearl Le.

My late uncle Danny Robinson, your timely words impacted my life.

Disclaimer:

The testimonies mentioned above are based on the women's own recollections

Contents

Dedication:	5
Acknowledgements:	5
Disclaimer:	5
Introduction	12
Message #1	14
"You were made to Prophesy"	14
A Message on Faith	14
His Maidservants:	14
…And they shall prophesy	16
Message #1 - You were made to prophesy!	17
The Gift of Prophecy	17
The Spirit of Prophecy	19
From Moses we learn	19
Continual Pouring	21
Message to My Maidservants:	22
Message #2	27
"Queen Under A Crown"	27
A Poem on self-love	27
Queen under a Crown	27
Message #3	33
"I have Preserved you!"	33
A Message on Separation	33
Message #3 - I have preserved you!	33
Manchester	35
I shall deliver their soul from death	37
A moment of grief	38

London	40
Jamaica	41
Bristol	42
Message to My Maidservants:	44
Message #4	**48**
"You were always enough!"	**48**
A Message on Self-Worth	**48**
Message #4 - You were always enough	49
Distractions	50
You were always enough!	54
Message to My Maidservants	55
Message #5	**60**
"I Am the Lifter of your Head"	**60**
A Message on Inner Peace	**60**
Message #5 - I Am the Lifter of your Head	61
Message to My Maidservants:	66
Message #6	**72**
"Run with Endurance!"	**72**
A Message on Perseverance	**72**
Message #6 - Run with Endurance	73
"Lay aside every weight"	75
The sin which so easily ensnares us	77
Mind Games?	78
Message to My Maidservants	82
Message #7	**86**
"Mother of Many Nations!"	**86**
A Message on Fruitfulness	**86**
Message #7 - Mother of Many Nations!	87
My Faith	89
Being a Single Mother	89

Breaking Free from Rejection	91
The Man Christ Jesus	92
Raising Children as a Christian	94
Add to your Faith Virtue, to Virtue …	95
…Knowledge	96
Perseverance through trials	98
Message to My Maidservants	101
Message #8	**106**
"No Eye Hath Seen"	**106**
A Message on Abundance	**106**
Message #8 - No eye hath seen	107
Five Keys to Living the Abundant Life:	108
1. Seek First the Kingdom:	108
2. Trust God in all Seasons:	109
3. Give Generously:	110
4. Maintain Perspective:	113
5. Take the Limits off your mind:	115
Message to My Maidservants:	116
Message #9	**121**
"For My Glory"	**121**
A Message on Purpose	**121**
Message #9 – For My Glory	122
I created you for you to worship Me	124
My story	124
What's my purpose?	125
Message to My Maidservants:	132
Message #10	**137**
"The Iron that Sharpens Her!"	**137**

A Message on Friendship **137**
    Iron is a metal 137
    Message #10 - The Iron that Sharpens Her 138
    # Friendship Goals: Which one are you? 140
    Message to My Maidservants 144

Message #11 .... **149**
A Servants Answered Prayer **149**
A Message on Love **149**
    Message #11 – A Servant's Answered Prayer 150
    Health Issues 151
    Chronic Fatigue Syndrome 155
    Marriage? 158
    The Courtship 161
    A Servants Answered Prayer 162
    Message to My Maidservants 163

Message #12 .... **167**
For Such a Time as This **167**
A Message on Destiny **167**
    Message #12 - For Such a Time as This: 168
    Pioneering 169
    First Stop Texas... 169
    New Mexico 170
    A dignified place to meet... 171
    Sunny San Francisco 174
    Radisson Hotel 175
    Prescott, Arizona 177
    Tucson, Arizona 178
    Parting the Red Sea 181
    For such a Time as this: 183

Message to My Maidservants:	185
About the Author	190

Introduction

When God gave me the title for this book, I deliberated over it for a while. God gave me the title for this book in 2018, but I didn't write it until the Covid-19 pandemic of 2020. London went into a period of lockdown in March 2020, that's when I sat down in the calm in the midst of the storm, that's when I started to write this book.

I pondered to myself about whether I had been through enough life experiences to write something like this: God's message to His maidservants. After much thought, time and prayer God showed me that in order to make this book even more applicable, as well as using illustrations from my own life I would go on to include features from other women in the field. In response, I invoked the testimonies of four amazing Christian Women from very different walks of life. I have added their testimonies to four different chapters of this book.

God inspired me to write this book, He inspired me to include the testimonies of other women of faith and He did this because He has things that He wants us to share with one another. The things that we go through in our Christian lives were never intended to be boxed away and put on a shelf. They were intended to be shared so that God can be glorified. In this book I want to share the things that God has laid upon my heart to share with you. As you read this book, I want you to hear God's voice for yourself. I want to address the longing for communion with our Heavenly Father, that we may come to know Him the way that He knows us.

Message to My Maidservants: From His Mouth to Our Ears is about cultivating a close relationship with the Father, through our Lord Jesus who made that possible.

I pray that as you churn through the pages of this book, you will be open to what the Spirit of God is speaking to you about. May your life always reflect the Father's heart towards you.

Love Desiri

Xoxo

Message #1
"You were made to Prophesy"
A Message on Faith

"¹And it shall come to pass in the last days, says God, That I will pour out of My Spirit on all flesh…¹⁸ And on My menservants and on My maidservants, I will pour out My Spirit in those days; And they shall prophesy."

Joel 2:28-29

God wants us to live and walk in unison with Him that we make speak according to His divine will and purpose.

His Maidservants:
In the book of Joel, God is talking about His maidservants. In the Hebrew Bible, the term handmaid is applied to a female servant who serves her mistress, as in the case of Hagar being described as Sarai's handmaid, Zilpah being Leah's handmaid and Bilhah as Rachel's handmaid. A maidservant is a female domestic servant. So, when God talks about *His* maidservants, He's talking about the women who serve in His House. He's talking about us.

The Last Days

God says that in the last days He will pour out His Spirit upon all of mankind; on His manservants and on His maidservants and they shall prophesy! See precious daughter, God wants to fill you with His Spirit.

In order to understand what God is saying here, we must fully grasp what is meant by the term, 'The Last Days.'

We learn from the book of Acts that on the Day of Pentecost, the Holy Spirit fell down upon the 120 saints who were gathered in one accord and there they began to, 'speak with other tongues, as the spirit gave them utterance,' (Acts 2:4). The crowd were not sure what to think; people thought that they were drunk with wine. The apostle Peter stood up under the anointing of the Holy Spirit and clarified the situation.

He explained that the people were not drunk and it was only about 9.00 A.M. What people were seeing amongst the saints was what was spoken of by the Prophet Joel:

> [17] 'And it shall come to pass in the last days, says God,
> That I will pour out of My Spirit on all flesh;
> Your sons and your daughters shall prophesy,
> Your young men shall see visions,
> Your old men shall dream dreams.
> [18] And on My menservants and on My maidservants
> I will pour out My Spirit in those days;
> And they shall prophesy.
> [19] I will show wonders in heaven above
> And signs in the earth beneath:
> Blood and fire and vapor of smoke.

²⁰ The sun shall be turned into darkness,
And the moon into blood,
Before the coming of the great and awesome day of the Lord.
²¹ And it shall come to pass
That whoever calls on the name of the Lord
Shall be saved.'

Acts 2: 17 -21

Here, the Prophet Joel is speaking about the happenings of, 'The Last Days.' Verse 20 makes reference to The Last Days being a time when, 'the sun shall be turned into darkness.' This is what happened when Jesus died on the cross, the gospel according to Luke tells us that the sun literally turned dark (Luke 23:45). By this we know that The Last Days are the days somewhere between Jesus' ascension into Heaven and His final return to Earth ('the great and awesome day of the Lord'). This means that you and I are currently living in The Last Days that the Prophet Joel spoke about.

Are we days from Jesus' final return? Are we years away? We don't know because to God *'one day is like a thousand years'* (2 Peter 3:8). However, Scripture tells us that in these last days there will be two amazing manifestations. First, God will pour His Spirit out on all mankind (menservants and maidservants) and second, "Whoever calls on the name of the Lord will be saved." (Act 2:21)

...And they shall prophesy

To prophesy means to speak what the Spirit of God is telling you to speak. So go ahead and speak what the Spirit of God is telling you to speak. In these last days, saith the Lord "I shall pour out of my spirit on all flesh." God wants us to walk in His Spirit.

Message #1 - You were made to prophesy!

I would like to begin by drawing a clear distinction between the gift of prophecy and the spirit of prophecy. All believers can prophesy, even though not all believers have the gift of prophesy.

The Gift of Prophecy

The spiritual gift of prophecy is an extraordinary and unique gift. Paul says in 1 Corinthians 14:1 to, "Pursue love, and earnestly desire the spiritual gifts, especially that you may prophesy."

The Greek word for the gift of prophecy is *propheteia* which is the ability to receive a divinely inspired message and deliver it to others in the church. He who prophesies speaks, edification and exhortation and comfort to men (1 Corinthians 14:3-4, 24-25). However, these words do not constitute the authoritative Word of God, but are the human interpretation of the revelation that was received. This gift of prophecy is a blessing to the church and should not be quenched or despised (1 Thessalonians 5:20). However, we are also told that we are not to believe every message; prophecies are spoken in human words through a human mind which is why they must be tested against the Scriptures (1 Thessalonians 5:20-21).

It was the year 2015. I remember the first prophetic word I spoke aloud to my local church:

"Yield to Me, and I will cleanse you from all unrighteousness, only dwell in My house and stay in my Word for I have esteemed by Word above My own name," says the Lord.

I felt liberated. However, I also had to face opposition. Some people found it difficult to understand and accept my gift and calling. So much so that some even tried to discourage me. They tried.

"I don't want you to prophesy!" says the voice of darkness. The devil works through weak and wounded people.

"You don't want me to do what?"

"I don't want you to prophesy," says that same oppressive voice.

"I bet you don't," said my inner voice.

If God calls you to it, then He will bring you through it.

"*For the gifts and the calling of God are irrevocable.*"
Romans 11:29

That satanic voice that tried to oppress me, had me in a state of frustration. I felt trapped; betrayed; I almost gave up, but I didn't. I had an amazing sister-friend that I could go and speak to at the time when this satanic voice was trying to oppress me. She told me to pray.
What do I do now God? You gave me this gift and now this voice of opposition has come against me and is trying to oppress me.

"He permitted no one to do them wrong; Yes, He rebuked kings for their sakes."
Psalms 105:14

God rebukes the voices of oppression. You were made to prophesy – so prophesy with boldness!

Then the voice came back again, like a ringing in my ear drum, "I don't want you to prophesy."

"I bet you don't."

When I first started ministering in this gift, I faced many struggles, people don't even know about.

So, what do you do when you've done all that you can? You do what God told you to do.

Oftentimes, people can fall into a state of negativity just based on the words of others – be careful what you tell yourself. Remember whose voice takes dominion. You have to get to a point where you're able to block out every voice contrary to the voice of God. Then you have to speak what the Spirit of God is telling you to speak. Do not speak doom and gloom over your life or the lives of others, instead speak the things that you want to see.

Get up every morning, prophesy every morning and prophesy with boldness.

The Spirit of Prophecy

From Moses we learn that the spirit of prophecy should not be restricted to Church leaders only:

> "Would God," he cried, "that all the Lord's people were prophets, and that the Lord would put His Spirit upon them!"
>
> **Numbers 11:29**

In Numbers 11:24-30, we have here the fulfilment of God's word to Moses, that he should have help in the government of Israel. God's Spirit came down and spoke to Moses, then God placed His Spirit on the seventy elders and they began to prophesy only when the Spirit rested upon them. Two of the elders, Eldad and Medad, did not go out to the tabernacle, they remained in the camp and prophesied there. A young man went and told Moses about this and Joshua – Moses' Assistant - told Moses to forbid these men from prophesying. Joshua saw this as a potential threat to Moses' authority as the leader. But Moses was of a different spirit, he was not afraid or intimidated by any such effects from that Spirit which God had put upon these men. In fact, Moses reproves Joshua, "Are you zealous for my sake?"

So far from silencing these two elders, and quenching the Spirit within them, Moses wishes that all the Lord's people were prophets, and that God would put His Spirit upon them. Here, Moses envisions the universal outpouring of the Holy Spirit that the Prophet Joel later goes on to proclaim - **Joel 2:28 – 29**.

Now we are living in the days of this outpouring.

The word 'prophecy' stems from the Greek work *prophemi,* which means to speak forth before. Thus, to prophesy is a proper term to describe the proclamation of God's Word in advance of events occurring. The bible is a prophetic book; God's Spirit is a spirit of prophecy, "Declaring the end from the beginning." (Isaiah 46:10)

Let's go back to the beginning, in Genesis 1, God created the whole world by speaking it into existence. The bible tells us in Genesis 1:2 that in the beginning, "The earth was without form and void; and darkness was on the face of the deep. And the Spirit of God was hovering over the faces of the water."

At this point, God didn't begin to speak about the darkness, He didn't complain or bring attention to the fact that the earth was without form and void. Instead, the bible tells us that God's Spirit was hovering over the faces of the water.

Then, in Genesis 1:3 He says, "*Let there be light and there was light."*

In the same chapter God says, *"Let there be a firmament in the midst of the waters, and let it divide the waters from the waters."* And so it was.

As God continued to speak those words, *"Let there be... let there be..."* so the Heavens and the earth were created.

God created the world by speaking it into existence. By this we know that the Spirit of God is a spirit of prophecy, *"Calling the things that be not as if they are."*

Romans 4:17

Continual Pouring

Before Jesus had ascended to heaven, He promised that he would give another, 'Helper'(John 14:16) that would be with us forever. That promise was fulfilled at Pentecost which can be seen in Acts 2.

"And they were all filled with the Holy Spirit and began to speak with other tongues, as the Spirit gave them utterance."

Acts 2:4

This at Pentecost, was God keeping His promise and pouring out His Spirit on all flesh. God's Spirit is the Spirit of Prophecy.

The outpouring of God's Spirit does not stop on this one Pentecost day; it continues. God says, *"I will pour out my Spirit on all people."*

The verb phrase [will pour] shows continual action. The Prophet Joel sees the Holy Spirit, 'poured out' in a way that signifies great abundance. Joel's prophecy trickles throughout generations.

We know that The Last Days, as proclaimed by the Prophet Joel have already begun because God's Spirit was poured out on the day of Pentecost. You and I live somewhere between Pentecost and Jesus' final return, this means that you and I are living in the Last Days!

Message to My Maidservants:
The bible tells us in Revelation 19:10 that the testimony of Jesus is the spirit of prophecy. This means that whenever you share the testimony of Jesus, whenever you share the gospel, that is actually prophetic. The whole bible is the testimony of Jesus - from Genesis to Revelation. This means that Scripture is prophetic, whenever you pray Scripture, speak Scripture or discuss Scripture you are entering into an avenue of the prophetic. Our verification for accurate prophecy is testing the Spirts and testing the prophecies to see whether they are from God.

Beloved, do not believe every spirit, but test the spirits, whether they are of God; because many false prophets have gone out into the world. **1 John 4:1**

How do we test the spirits? God's Word is our verification. We test the Spirit by seeing whether it aligns with the Word of God. When the Word of God is engraved within, you will be able to test your own utterances.

By this you know the Spirit of God: Every spirit that confesses that Jesus Christ has come in the flesh is of

God.

1 John 4:2

When you feel led to speak your words if they are inspired by the Spirit, they will always testify and manifest the heart of the Father that was revealed by His Son, Jesus. God has poured out the Holy Spirit, this is why you can prophesy in these last days. We are God's image bearers on this earth and our lives were created to bring Him glory.
God's Spirit has equipped you, so go ahead, speak what the Spirit of God tells you to speak.

You were made to prophesy, therefore prophesy with boldness.

Reflection & Prayer

Message #1 You were made to Prophesy

Message to My Maidservants

Message #2 "Queen Under A Crown"
A Poem on self-love

Queen under a Crown

*Woman thou art worthy!
Crafted by the master's hand
engraved so perfectly.*

***Sculpted by a blacksmith's tools
refined in a furnace full of precious jewels
Queen under a crown and so worthy to be
Chiselled by the master's hand
Carved so perfectly***

*Your outer layer sanded down
with a rod of perfection
A compass in your mind for
the Lord's direction.
Folded and kept away by
your father's protection.
But you lost many gems along the way
Now your crown is crooked
much to my dismay
And when it rains, I shed tears
for how far you stray
And the man that you're with
is not the one I ordained*

*Yet you bow your head and keep
silent cos you feel so ashamed.
Queen fix your crown*

**Sculpted by a blacksmith's tools
refined in a furnace full of precious jewels
Queen under a crown and so worthy to be
Chiselled by the master's hand
Carved so perfectly**

*You left pearls and precious
gems in a bed of immorality
Pieces of your broken crown
now wallow in self-pity
My compass replaced by
your insecurity. Queen!
You lost pieces of the crown that
were perfectly formed by Me.*

*I imparted you with self-esteem
And a deep sense of worth
Daughter of a king
My very image on this earth.*

*Listen to Jeremiah:
Before I formed you in your
mother's womb, I knew you.
I twisted and fashioned
every hair on your head
And I gave clear instructions
for you to be led
I have a man that loves you
the way that I desire
But you resolve for short cuts
a crown in the mire*

**Sculpted by a blacksmith's tools
refined in a furnace full of precious jewels**

**Queen under a crown and so worthy to be
Chiselled by the master's hand
Carved so perfectly**

*My unfailable plan was laid out
for your peace of mind
Yet anxiety has you bound as
you look around and behind
Your filled with self-doubt and
fall prey to comparison
You'll never win at being her
For I made you to be you.*

*But why did you ignore the
last part of my manual,
You settle for a life that you
weren't made to handle,
For I did not simply say that you
should love your neighbour
I said love thy neighbour
as thy love thyself.*

**Sculpted by a blacksmith's tools
refined in a furnace full of precious jewels
Queen under a crown and so worthy to be
Chiselled by the master's hand
In my image I made thee!**

Reflection & Prayer

✧ ❀ ✧

Message #2 Queen Under a Crown

Message to My Maidservants

Message #3 "I have Preserved you!" A Message on Separation

"Behold, the eye of the Lord is on those who fear Him, on those who hope in His mercy, To deliver their soul from death and to keep them alive in famine."

Psalms 33:18-19

God wants us to know that in times of separation, or what we perceive to be times of separation, He has *preserved* us.

Preservation is an abstract noun, it means the act of keeping something the same or preventing it from being damaged, lost or injured. When something is preserved, it is protected from becoming decomposed, disintegrated and spoiled. God wants us to know that in times of separation He has preserved us.

Message #3 - I have preserved you!

Her name is Cheryl, the year is 1998, she is 21 years old, she has been married for just over 2 years and she is four months pregnant. God is about to call her away from her place of comfort and send her and her new husband out into a foreign land.

"Before I got married my husband told me that he felt God had called him to go and preach the gospel in the mission field, he wanted to be a missionary Pastor which meant I had to prepare to be a Pastors wife. I knew that there were many other couples in our church that wanted to be sent out onto the mission field as well so in my mind I calculated that it would be at least three or four years after the marriage before it got to our turn.

I exhaled at this point in the conversation believing that I had plenty of time to prepare myself. I was nineteen years old and excited to be getting married to the love of my life, there was plenty of time to worry about his plans of being a Pastor; I was fine with that. We got married in June 1995, however, things didn't go according to *my* 5-year plan – not at all.

It was November 1997; we were at our church conference and our Pastor announced us as the first couple to be sent out to go and Pastor a church in Manchester. I couldn't believe it, I had been married for just over two years, this was not how it was supposed to go! It was so unexpected, I mean no one at the conference really knew who we were as a couple, I don't think anyone was expecting us to be the first ones to go. This was not my plan. Well, as the old Jamaican saying goes, "man is planning and God is wiping out."

There are many plans in a man's heart, Nevertheless the LORD's counsel—that will stand.
Proverbs 19:21

What could I do at this point? I was married, I was 4 months pregnant; God had called us to leave behind everything we ever knew and go out and pioneer a church in the south of Manchester.

Manchester

Although the announcement was made in November 1997, we didn't officially open the church in Manchester until March 1998, by this point I was eight months pregnant. Moving to Manchester was a daunting experience for me, I didn't know anyone there. I'm a social butterfly you see, I just love to be around people. In my mind I felt that Manchester was just going to be me, my husband and my pregnant self!

The January before we moved to Manchester was probably the worst in terms of coming to terms with what was happening, my husband left for Manchester at the beginning of January and I didn't join him until the end. It was there in our 9th floor, two-bedroom flat in Elephant and Castle that I was left alone with my thoughts and feelings. My body was tied up in knots of nervousness and excitement at the same time. I was excited about what God was going to do with my husband and I in Manchester, I kept myself occupied thinking about our house and the people that we were going to meet out there. But I was nervous because I didn't know what to expect. I dreaded the prospect of leaving behind my friends, my family and my church.

I mean what if we didn't make friends out there? What if no one wanted to come to our church? These were the questions that occupied my mind – besides who were we anyway? What if we were leaving behind our vibrant church, our friends, family and everything we knew to go to a derelict place where no one wanted to attend? Nervous excitement is like being at the peak curve of a rollercoaster! You know what's about to happen but you're still holding your breath in anticipation.

At this point in my life my church was my family. Not to mention I was leaving my mother and two younger brothers behind in London as well. I had to tell myself to stop thinking the worst; that it was all going to work out. I had to remind myself that God had called us to this life and He was going to see us through. I couldn't let anything stand in the way.

He who loves father or mother more than Me is not worthy of Me. And he who loves son or daughter more than Me is not worthy of Me.

Mark 10:34

The month that I spent alone in London was a time of reflection for me, initially when I said that I would go to Manchester I was doing it for my husband, but during this time alone in January I had to get something of my own from God. It was then that I gained a new appreciation for my church, you see I was saved at a young age and I grew up in church so I had an experience of giving into the work of the kingdom of God.

In my place of solitude, I gained a deeper perspective on the importance of giving, that was when I realised how many people were trusting in us. They had invested in us not just spiritually – with their prayers - but financially as well, people were giving money towards us being sent to pioneer this church in an area of Manchester. We had invested in ourselves and it was time for us to branch out and do the work that God had called us to do.

Reality hit me when I arrived in Manchester, prior to that I was in preparation mode. When I stepped off that train and set foot into the City of Manchester that was when that fear of separation transformed into a frightening reality - it was me, my husband, God and the devil! It might sound strange, me saying that I experienced such a strong feeling of separation, because I wasn't alone, alone – I was out there with my husband. Having my husband by my side definitely made things much easier, but leaving behind everything I had ever known still made me feel lonely. I was away from my mother, my brothers and my church family. I felt the sense of separation, it was real. London was my home; it was all I'd ever known as a Christian.

I think separation in itself is a form of loss but grief hit me when I got to Manchester.

I shall deliver their soul from death[1]

When we moved to Manchester, it wasn't all comfort and country walks as some might imagine. Leaving the hustle and bustle of London I tried to comfort myself with the expectation of a quiet countryside home where we could focus on building our church and doing works for God. In fact, we moved to a dangerous area in south Manchester called Moss Side; we ended up staying on the most notorious street in Moss Side: Claremont Street. I remember there being a gang feud on our street between 'The Gooch Gang' and 'The Doddington

---

[1] Psalms 33:19 To deliver their soul from death, And to keep them alive in famine NKJV

Gang.' The gangs ran the street, Claremont was not a nice place to live – not at all - it was full of robberies and daily drug dealings. I remember hearing stories of students strolling down Claremont Road and getting robbed right there in broad daylight. This was a regular occurrence. This is where we lived and this is where God wanted us to pioneer a church! Despite all the mis-happenings around Moss Side I still had to go about my day-to-day business with my heavily pregnant self. Despite living in such dangerous surroundings, nothing bad ever happened to me in Moss Side. I have preserved you.

I still felt lonely out there though, I didn't have anyone to go and hang out with whilst my husband was out working, we didn't know anyone in Manchester. So instead, I began writing down the names of people on my street on which we lived and I began praying for them by name. My prayer life changed during this period because that's all I had.

Shortly after we moved to Manchester, the baby came, he was born on 3rd May 1998 and we called him Brandon. I didn't have many visitors when Brandon was born, once again it was just me, my husband and our new-born son.

A moment of grief
Things took a turn for the worse when I was told that my mother had a nervous breakdown and had to be taken into hospital.

I started praying and fasting:

"God what will happen to my brothers?"

God answered me. Mum was admitted to hospital for six months. I was twenty-two years old and I found myself as the Legal Guardian of a nine-year-old and a thirteen-year-old boy.

Sitting in my living room next to one of the most notorious streets in south Manchester, I felt like the weight of my life was too heavy to hold up. Pioneering a church; looking after two young boys; a new baby and having no extra financial support for my brothers. It was November 1998; we had been in Manchester for less than a year and my life had changed so much. It was by the Grace of God that I was so able to survive.

God gave me insight and wisdom beyond my years because at twenty – two years old I was dealing with a heavy load that I wasn't quite sure how to carry. My brothers lived with us for a year; I had to deal with social workers, doctors and housing all whilst raising my new born baby.

After six months, mum got out of the hospital and I was able to move her over to Manchester. By the Grace of God mum got a place a few doors down from where we lived. My brothers moved back in with mum and we stayed in Manchester for 4 years.

Eventually, the church got up and running and we had a few people attending. In terms of my own mental health, I was usually fine during the week but I started to experience anxiety on Sundays. Looking back, I feel like this was partly due to the area and our surroundings but also, I guess I never really got used to being away from our own church. There I could just attend and serve; here I was the Pastor's wife and I guess I became anxious about what to expect at each service. I was worried about whether people would attend the church, whether we would be able to support ourselves and even whether I had enough in me to pour out into the women that attended the church. I guess I did tend to overthink too much back then. This was our first experience in pioneering.

Anxiety eased off during the week but crept back upon me every Sunday. I found myself having constant mind battles. There was nothing I could do, I just had to pray it through.

[6] Be anxious for nothing, but in everything by prayer and supplication, with thanksgiving, let your requests be made known to God; [7] and the peace of God, which surpasses all understanding, will guard your hearts and minds through Christ Jesus.
Philippians 4:6-8

London
In 2002, we left Manchester because we got called back to our mother church in London to become the Assistant Pastors. This for me was a time of refreshing, as far as I was concerned, I was back home again. London is my home and it is my place of comfort! But we didn't stay home for too long though, God had other plans. We spent two years in London then it was separation time again.

Wolverhampton
In June 2004 we were asked to take over a pioneer church in the city of Wolverhampton. This was a lot easier for me to transition into than when we initially got sent to Manchester. God had used that time in Manchester to prepare my heart for this life of servitude. Our time in Wolverhampton wasn't short lived, we spent seven years there.

Wolverhampton wasn't too difficult for me to adapt to; it was my place of comfort – I found favour there. Our church grew quickly and as soon as God sent ladies into the church, I began to pour into them. I would have women's prayer meetings and fellowships with these ladies. I found comfort and peace in Wolverhampton; I could be that social butterfly once again. Not long after moving to Wolverhampton, my mother also came to join us. Mum stayed with us for a bit - with my younger brother - before she got her own place. I found it difficult being separated from my mum; I found myself constantly worried about how she was going to cope. Having her nearby gave me peace of mind.

Jamaica

After spending seven years in Wolverhampton, my husband and I were sent to pioneer a church in Mandeville, Jamaica. That was the real test of separation for me. When we went to Jamaica my mother did not speak to me for three years, she felt like I had left her. She was so used to coming with me everywhere we went, but not this time. Isolation. Jamaica was my place of isolation. I was on sabbatical for 9 months.

When we started the church all the people that were coming in were young men, there were no ladies for me to pour into for the first 9 months. Fear would captivate me at times; I was afraid to drive for the first three years of living in Mandeville. Isolation, separation and sabbatical – that was me for three whole years. I had to learn to adapt to my surroundings. Adaptation in separation is really important. I had to learn how to be a chameleon and I had to learn fast.

It was during my time of isolation and sabbatical in Jamaica that I had to come to terms with my own mind battles. Mental illness runs in my family. I didn't think it affected me but in that place of separation the thought of not being able to cope began to push me over the edge. I didn't think I could cope with Jamaica when I first got there. There wasn't anything anyone could say or do to convince me otherwise – I just had to face up to the thoughts in my own mind.

"When I am afraid, I will trust in You."

That was the Word that came back to encourage me, over the years whenever people had given me a Word they would say, "When I am afraid, I will trust in you." So that's what I had to do. I had to learn to trust God with my thought life.

Casting down arguments and every high thing that exalts itself against the knowledge of God, bringing every thought into captivity to the obedience of Christ,

2 Corinthians 10:5

There were times when fear would come and attack my mind, fear would tell me quite bluntly "You're not going to cope." I took my thoughts to God in prayer, I've learnt that when my thoughts are going to a certain place to take them to God. Faith over fear. That same prophetic utterance came back to me like light piercing through cracks in the darkness - *when I am afraid, I will trust in You Lord*.

Bristol
We spent six years in Mandeville, Jamaica before returning to the United Kingdom to take over a church in Bristol in 2017. I quickly adapted to living in Bristol and

I even started up a lady's prayer group. After the 18 months stopover in Bristol, we returned back home to London again.

We left London in 1998 and returned in 2019, that means we spent 22 years travelling across the globe, separated from our friends and family. Every single experience helped me to develop endurance and longevity.

Manchester was a dark place but that's where my faith developed; Wolverhampton was my place of comfort, that's where I started teaching in the children's church, I learnt how to drive and I started working in the community; Jamaica was my place of isolation – my mum didn't come with me to Jamaica. God eventually brought me safely back to my home town - well my temporary home - London.

Mum is still in Wolverhampton until this day, but I'm ok with that. Being in Jamaica set me free from attachment to my mum that I didn't even realise that I had.

There were some things that I thought I couldn't cope with mentally, but through my separation experiences God has shown me that I can.

"Behold, the eye of the Lord is on those who fear Him, on those who hope in His mercy, to deliver their soul from death and to keep them alive in famine."

Psalms 33:18-19

For us, living in Mandeville Jamaica was a place of 'famine,' there were times when we had to struggle with the shortage of water and electricity. But through it all God kept us. I learnt how to survive without my family, I had to learn to adapt to people, places and foreign cultures. God kept His promise of sending people ahead of us, I remember a 15-year-old girl that I met in Manchester, she was one of the first young girls to get saved; she is married now serving in the church in Wolverhampton.

I'm back to where we started now, London. Looking back over our 22-year journey of separation I realise that God taught me something new in every land I stepped foot on. There was strength in the place of death, growth in the place of comfort and adaptation in the place of separation. Even in our most trying moments, God did not allow harm to come to us. He preserved us."

Message to My Maidservants:
Sometimes we perceive separation as a negative experience, it can have negative connotations in the sense that to be separated means to be kept apart, to be isolated or to be singled out. In reality, God often uses times of separation to teach us things, he uses times of separation to help us to grow. I have found that some of my greatest moments and lessons during my salvation have actually occurred when I was in my quiet time and alone with God.

But what God wants us to know is that in these times and seasons of separation, in our darkest moments, when we feel alone or when we are taken away from everything we've ever known, God is with us and He says – I have preserved you!

In times of separation, know that I have preserved you.

Message #3 I have preserved you!

Reflection & Prayer

◇ ❀ ◇

Message to My Maidservants

Message #3 I have preserved you!

Message #4
"You were always enough!"
A Message on Self-Worth

"But God demonstrates His own love toward us, in that while we were still sinners, Christ died for us."
Romans 5:8

'Self-worth' is a noun often used to refer to an individual's perception of how much value they place upon themselves. The Cambridge dictionary defines self-worth as, 'the value you give to your life and achievements.' Some people derive their sense of value and self-worth from work, for others it may be educational achievements, some may find self-worth by seeking validation from people. This can also lead to imbalanced and unhealthy relationships.

Oftentimes, our sense of self-worth can be affected by many situations and circumstances that we find ourselves in. There are times in life when we face challenging situations. If our sense of self-worth is not rooted in firm foundations then these situations can shake us off course and get us walking down the wrong path. Some adverse situations are set up to make us believe certain lies about ourselves. In these moments we need to step back and remember who we are, God's special possession.

He called us out of darkness.

In fact, God demonstrated the value that He places upon us with action, the action of a cross stained by blood. While we were still sinners, Christ died for us. This should give us great confidence, knowing that even in our worst state God purchased us at a high price.

The adjective "sinners," means that whilst we were still, outlaws, revellers and immoral, Christ died. Sometimes we get ourselves into situations in life; we allow these situations to shape us. We allow people's words, their opinions, even their rejection to shape us. We have to be careful where we place our worth and value. God calls us, "His special possession." Christ has put His value on us.

"But you are a chosen people, a royal priesthood, a holy nation, God's special possession..."

1 Peter 2:9 (NIV)

In this message on self-worth God wants you to know that you were always enough and you are worth it.

Message #4 - You were always enough

We need to constantly be aware of our worth and who we are in Christ because there are many things that can come against us as women in God's Kingdom. In particular, in seasons that precede significant breakthroughs, there can be many distractions and things that come against us in order to bring about a hindrance. Make no mistake, these things are sent to distract you from your destiny.

When Daniel prayed in Chapter 10, his answer was delayed but the Angel of the Lord still visited him and gave him strength.

11 He said to me, "Daniel, you are a man who is highly precious. Consider carefully the words that I am about to say to you. Stand up, for I have now been sent to you." And when he had said this to me, I stood up trembling.

12 "Do not be afraid, Daniel," he said, "for from the first day that you purposed to understand and to humble yourself before your God, your words were heard, and I have come in response to them.

13 However, the prince of the kingdom of Persia opposed me for twenty-one days...

Daniel 10: 11 -13

The Angel of the Lord faced opposition for 21 days, but he still brought his message to Daniel. Although things may come against you and try to hinder you, remember that you are highly precious to God and He has the answer to your prayers!

Distractions

Love yourself enough to walk away from places, people and situations that don't value you. No arguments, no qualms, just walk.

We have to be able to recognise counterfeit friendships and relationships in our lives. Counterfeit goods look like the real thing, may even sound like the real thing, but they don't hold the same value, they have an appearance of quality but no substance to them. Counterfeit goods can only be sold next to other counterfeits; they can't co-exist with the real thing because the comparison will be too obvious. Only those that don't know what the real thing looks like will fall for a counterfeit.

I have learned that a lot of trouble and pain can be avoided in life if we just follow this one simple rule:

The *first* time someone shows you who they are, believe them!

I've come to realise that there's purpose in the counterfeit too. God wants to know whether you will recognise the real thing when you see it. Are your prayers specific enough? This doesn't have to just be in relationships but anything, new job, new house, dealing with difficult people. Are we really getting alone with God and telling Him what we want? Or are we just generalising our prayers to a point where we can't even recognise whether the thing that came into our life is an answer to a prayer.

You have to know your worth; be secure in who you are and realise when you could be settling for less than God's best. Be the woman that God created you to be.

Timely Words

It was the year 2015, I still remember the words that my Late Uncle Danny Robinson spoke to me one morning after prayer. 2015 was a strange, transitional year and his timely words impacted my life.

"You are not just an ordinary girl, you're a Christian girl."

I heard these words so loud that they became engraved in my spirit and I can't unhear them until this day. I still remember his slim, dark, face looking right at me; his eyes lighting up as he spoke these words with a gleaming smile across his face. It was about a month or so after my 30th birthday and I remember Uncle Danny telling me that people would never know my age by looking at me. I don't think he knew my age either, he never really asked me so when I told him that day, he just kind of shook his head and laughed.

Then he said, "But you would never know that by looking at you."

This was just one of our early morning conversations, Uncle Danny always spoke to me after our morning prayer sessions and he often gave me words of encouragement. Uncle Danny was being quite comical that day. I think he was trying to find out whether I had met anyone or had 'news' for him yet. Growing up in church or just being a single Christian woman can be difficult at times especially during the time of your late 20's and 30's. People are so quick to try and tell you what you should be doing or where you should be at by now. Without clear understanding of God's plans you can even start to worry about missing certain milestones.

*"A (wo)man's heart plans (her) way,
But the Lord directs her steps."*

Proverbs 16:9

As women in general, we face many pressures from society and from those around us to conform to certain standards. I remember Uncle Danny laughing and reminding me that I should continue to serve God as I was doing.

"I don't want you to think, ok so thirty, right so desperation," then he cracked that long distinctive laugh that makes you want to laugh right along with him.

It was so funny that Uncle Danny would make such light-hearted jokes about something like that and then laugh afterwards because in reality that is how many people think. Many women fear getting into the category of the 'over 30's' and not being married yet, this could come from internal fears or ideas that have been projected upon us by society.

Uncle Danny spoke with such conviction that his words became engraved:

"You are not just an ordinary girl, You're a Christian girl!"

He was telling me to remember who I was. Our identity is found in Christ. If you're a Christian that means that Christ lives in you. He lives in you! Pray that when people come around you something of Him rubs off on them. Call me an idealist but I don't believe that anyone can come into contact with a Holy Ghost filled Christian and not have their life impacted in some way. If Christ lives in you that means that your body is the temple of the Holy Spirit. You were always enough and you are worth it!

The Psalmist said:

"I've been young, and now am old; yet never have I seen the righteous forsaken or his descendants begging bread."

Psalms 37:25

Let's face it, not everyone will see you the way that God sees you. It's not every piece of advice that someone speaks to you that you must take on board – be careful who you get close to and who you let speak into your life.

Don't let anybody put a label on you because Christ has put a value on you. I've had occasions where people have tried to label me with their opinion, perceptions or restrictions. In situations like this it is easy to get side-tracked, start to feel low down or wonder why me... right? God is faithful. In situations where I have gone through what seems to be a moment of irritation or disappointment, God has sent people to speak timely words or just to remind me that my presence counts.

"For I know the thoughts that I think toward you, says the Lord, thoughts of peace and not of evil, to give you a future and a hope."

Jeremiah 29:11

Although things may come against you and try to hinder you, remember that you are highly precious to God and He has the answer to your prayers!

You were always enough!

In times of discouragement, God wants you to remember who you are! Place your sense of self-worth in Christ and never forget how valuable you are to Him. Make no mistake about this woman of God, the devil sends counterfeits. He sends counterfeit people, counterfeit advice and counterfeit situations. But God is faithful, so keep on praying and passing those tests; God has great plans in store for your life. There are times in my salvation, even at times where I myself had been too naive to see what was really going on around me, God stepped in and rescued me from people, places and situations that did not fit my destiny.

If you continue to seek God then He will show you the things that are for you and the things that are not.

He opens the door that no man can shut and He shuts the door that no man can open.

Isaiah 22:22

There are some situations in life that we may not have been strong enough to walk away from by ourselves, perhaps because there were things that we couldn't quite see clearly at the time. It is in those situations that God says, He had to do it!

"I had to close that door because I couldn't allow you to settle."

Message to My Maidservants

God wants you to know that you were always enough and you are worth it. You were purchased at a high price – you are valuable to Him.

Before you were born, you were enough, we know this because God says in **Jeremiah 1:5**, *"Before I formed you in the womb, I knew you."*

Before you knew Christ you were enough, we know this because God says in **Romans 5:8**, *"While we were still sinners Christ died for us."*

Right now, if you're a Christian that means that Christ lives in you. He lives in you.

Or do you not know that your body is the temple of the Holy Spirit who is in you, whom you have from God, and you are not your own?

1 Corinthians 6:19

Your identity is found in Christ, you belong to God. When you know the love of God in your life, you will never be a prisoner to human validation. God depicts His love for us in action. Imagery. The image of a cross – stained by blood. God knows our worth, we need to know our worth.

"For you were bought at a price; therefore, glorify God in your body and in your spirit, which are God's."

1 Corinthians 6:20

The word of God reminds us of our value. Special enough to die for. Always remember who you are and Whose you are. You were purchased at a high price. That God Himself would step out of His heavenly throne room and humble Himself to death, even the death of the cross. **2 Corinthians 5:15** tells us that, *"He died for all, that those who live should live no longer for themselves, but for Him who died for them and rose again."*

By this we know that our body and our spirits belong to God.

To know Christ is to know your worth. You were always enough and you are worthy.

Message #4 You were always enough!

Reflection & Prayer

◇ ❀ ◇

Message to My Maidservants

Message #4 You were always enough!

Message #5
"I Am the Lifter of your Head"
A Message on Inner Peace

But You, O LORD, *are* a shield for me, my glory and the One who lifts up my head.

Psalms 3:3

God wants us to overcome the battles in our mind; we were called to walk in freedom.

'Peace,' is an abstract noun. It is a state of tranquillity but it is also an intangible asset. The Cambridge Dictionary describes peace as, 'freedom from war and violence.' It is the state of not being interrupted or annoyed by worry, problems, noise, or unwanted actions. The word 'Inner,' is an adjective which means, 'inside or contained within something else.' Therefore, when we talk about 'inner peace,' we mean an internal state of freedom from wars - otherwise known as mind battles.

Many times, we can get bogged down by mind battles. Oftentimes, people don't want to talk about issues such as anxiety and depression - especially as Christians – it's almost unheard of. As a disclaimer, this is not a chapter on mental health nor is it an attempt to provide any sort of medical diagnosis on depression. There is a major and complex difference between clinical depression and feeling depressed or going through low times.

This is a chapter about experiencing inner peace, in the midst of difficult circumstances. Anxiety can be caused by a variety of things such as meditating on the wrong words or dealing with the process of unanswered prayers. These things can play on our minds or be triggered by new events. This can lead to an endless cycle of tiresome mind battles.

God sees and He says, *"cast(ing) all your anxiety on Him, because He cares for you."*

1 Peter 5:7

In this message on inner peace God wants you to know that He is the lifter of your head.

Message #5 - I Am the Lifter of Your Head

From the life of Hannah, a maidservant of the Lord. Her name is Hannah, the year is 1200 BC and she's been asking God for something.

Hannah was married to a man named Elkanah who had two wives. Hannah was the first, but she had no children so he took on a second wife called Peninnah. Peninnah had children for Elkanah. In the 11th century BC, it was considered customary to take on a second wife when the first wife could not bear the fruit of the womb. Despite the fact that Hannah was unable to bear children, it was obvious that Elkanah loved her more than Peninnah. Every year Elkanah travelled from his home town to offer his sacrifices at the temple of the Lord. The temple of the Lord was in a place called Shiloh. This was where the tabernacle was set up. Whenever Elkanah returned from Shiloh to distribute his wealth, he would give a portion to Peninnah his wife and to all her sons and daughters but to Hannah he would give a double portion. The double portion could be said to represent a portion for the sons she did not have.

Although Hannah was barren, Peninnah was jealous of the fact that Hannah found more favour in the sight of Elkanah. As a result, she tormented Hannah and provoked her to misery because the Lord had closed Hannah's womb. Hannah was not provoked to anger over the taunting, instead she was broken. We could even say that Hannah was depressed.

There was a deep sense of inner turmoil that consumed Hannah from the inside out. Every day Hannah had to look at Peninnah swanning around the house with her children, being reminded of the fact that she herself was barren. Hannah hung her head low. During Hannah's generation, women who could not bear children were considered as cursed by God. Hannah's circumstances undoubtedly robbed her of inner peace.

This continued on for many years, Hannah would go to the Lord's house at Shiloh and ask God to open up her womb. Every year that Hannah remained barren, she had to deal with Peninnah spitefully mocking her. Hannah wept, she cried in excruciating tears but her tears led her to a place of fasting and prayer. Hannah was a prayer warrior, a mighty woman. From this we learn that our response is critical. Hannah did not justify or validate the taunts of her enemies, she understood it wasn't a physical battle that she was facing. Hannah took it to God. May God grant us the grace to respond to situations of inner conflict with the same understanding that Hannah did.

"Why do you weep dearest wife?" her husband affectionately enquired of her.

It was obvious why Hannah was weeping; she had been asking God every year to bless her with a child and her prayers remained unanswered. In addition, Hannah had to suffer and be taunted daily by Peninnah whose womb God had opened.

Elkanah, not understanding the depth of Hannah's inner turmoil, continued to enquire about the route of her distress.

"Why do you not eat? And why is your heart grieved? Am I not better to you than ten sons?"

1 Samuel 1:8

Elkanah wanted Hannah to be satisfied with him but Hannah's heart longed for a child. In 1 Samuel 1:10 we read that Hannah was 'in bitterness of soul,' because the Lord had not answered her prayer. As Hannah continued to pray, she wept in agony.

Hannah experienced the severest form of inner turmoil. Only God knows what was going through her mind at the time. Being unable to bear children was the ultimate form of humiliation for a married Hebrew woman in those times. She had no one to carry on her husband's name or pass on his estate to. This led to humiliation and insecurity, Hannah would've felt like nothing she did was good enough. This was a situation over which Hannah had no control, only God could take away her shame. Hannah cried out to God for something only He could do.

"Be anxious for nothing, but in everything by prayer and supplication, with thanksgiving let your requests be made known to God."

Philippians 4:6

In 1 Samuel 1:11, Hannah made a vow to the Lord in her distress. At her wits end, Hannah couldn't take her barrenness anymore. She made her request known to God:

"O Lord of hosts, if You will indeed look on the affliction of Your maidservant and remember me, and not forget Your maidservant, but will give your maidservant a male child, then I will give him to the Lord all the days of his life."

The repetition of the noun 'maidservant,' within Hannah's petition to the Lord could be representative of her subservience and dependence upon God.

Hannah continued to intercede for a child with intensity. We learn in 1 Samuel 1:13 that as Hannah prayed, she spoke in her heart only. Her words were not heard except between herself and the Lord. There was a priest called Eli who watched Hannah as she prayed. Her lips did not move so he thought that she was drunk.

"How long will you be drunk?" Eli questioned Hannah.

Hannah told Eli that she was a woman of deep sorrow and she had poured out her soul before the Lord. Hannah shared her grief with Eli the priest, once again referring to herself as a maidservant. Eli conversed with her and sent her on her way in peace praying that the God of Israel may grant the petition which she had asked of Him. That day Hannah left the presence of Eli and she ate and was no longer sad. Hannah was no longer downcast because the Lord had answered her prayers. The following morning Elkanah and Hannah woke up early and worshipped before the Lord. Not too long afterwards, Hannah conceived a male child and called his name Samuel.

Hannah kept her vow to the Lord, when Samuel was two or three years old, she took Samuel along with her offerings and went back to the Lord's temple in Shiloh. Hannah brought the child to Eli the priest and gave him unconditionally to the Lord. The Lord heard Hannah's cry, took mercy on her and granted her petition so that she may overcome the social disgrace associated at that time with barrenness.

Samuel grew up in Shiloh with Eli the priest. Hannah and Elkanah would go and see him every year when they went to make their yearly sacrifice. Eli continued to pray and bless the couple. Some time after Samuel had grown, the Lord blessed Hannah again so that she conceived three more sons and two daughters. We don't hear about Peninnah again after this point in the story.

"And the child Samuel grew in stature and in favour both with the Lord and men."

1 Samuel 1:26

Hannah was able to respond in the right way to a situation that had no doubt caused her great inner turmoil and had the ability to rob her of her peace. Hannah's turmoil was caused by constant humiliation and taunting. But Hannah did not run. Oftentimes we may choose to run away from situations that rob us of our peace. But Hannah stayed in her place.

"My heart rejoices in the Lord; My horn is exalted in the Lord. I smile at my enemies, because I rejoice in Your salvation."

1 Samuel 2:1

Hannah was God's maidservant. Her enemies taunted her but in her distressed state she turned to the Lord in fervent prayer. Lord hear my cry. The bible says in Psalms 34:17 that the righteous cry out and the Lord hears; He delivers them from all of their troubles. From this we learn that the absence of inner peace can be caused by many factors in life. Oftentimes the situations that bring us low are out of our control. God wants us to remember Him in situations that are out of control because He is always there, even in the presence of our enemies.

Message to my Maidservants:

In Christ you can have inner peace in the midst of your storms knowing that God is the lifter of your head. You don't need to run from situations that cause inner turmoil. Notice how Hannah did not run from the presence of Peninnah and the Hebrew women who may have looked down on her due to her situation. We can stay in our place and trust the Lord.

Sometimes the things in life that are the most difficult to admit that we are dealing with can be the very things that are hindering us from entering into the next stage of all that God has in store for us. Hannah had to admit that she was struggling; she had to admit her grief and pour out her heart before God. There's a battle that takes place inside the mind of every believer, the flesh warring against the spirit. Whichever side we choose to follow, will impact how we respond in situations of emotional uproar.

"For the flesh lusts against the Spirit, and the Spirit against the flesh; and these are contrary to one another, so that you do not do the things that you wish."

Galatians 5:17

Mind battles are often caused by a conflict of voices in our heads. We must decide who we are going to listen to, choose to follow the Words of Christ. If we are going to enter into all that God has in store for us then we're going to have to let go of some things and be honest before God. Sometimes we have to go back in order to go forward, other times we just have to pray, speak truth and trust God. In times of emotional turmoil, when you're on the brink of depression or you are experiencing inner conflict, God wants you to turn to Him and meditate on His Word.

When a person is going through inner turmoil, it can affect their whole state of being and even their posture. When you feel discouraged, you may not want to look at or face people. This may be because you feel shame or just because you don't want people to know what you're going through. But God says in Hebrews 12:2 that we should be, "looking unto Jesus, the author and finisher of our faith..." If we are going to keep looking unto Jesus then that means our head needs to be up. The Lord helps His people in times of trouble.

But You, O Lord are a shield for me, My glory and the One who lifts up my head.

Psalms 3:3

Message #5 I Am the Lifter of your Head

Reflection & Prayer

Message to My Maidservants

Message #5 I Am the Lifter of your Head

Message #6
"Run with Endurance!"
A Message on Perseverance

Therefore, we also, since we are surrounded by so great a cloud of witnesses, let us lay aside every weight, and the sin which so easily ensnares us, and let us run with endurance the race that is set before us.
Hebrews 12:1

Who is this 'cloud of witnesses' spoken about in the book of Hebrews? I imagine the cloud of witnesses to be those who have gone before, those whose lives are a testimony of the fruit of endurance. Jesus went before us and His life is the greatest testimony of endurance as laid out in Hebrews 12:2.

"...looking unto Jesus, the author and finisher of our faith, who for the joy that was set before Him endured the cross..."

Endurance is a noun; the Cambridge Dictionary defines endurance as the ability to keep doing something difficult, unpleasant, or painful for a long time. Jesus endured suffering for us, He endured the cross, His life is our witness. In this message of perseverance God wants us to know that even within the difficult, unpleasant or painful times of our walks we must keep going; run with endurance!

Message #6 - Run with Endurance

What do you normally do when you are in physical or emotional pain? What do you do when you're experiencing heartache? Do you just give up and throw in the towel or do you push through the pain and keep on going? What is heartache anyway?

The dictionary definition of heartache is emotional pain or distress; sorrow; grief; anguish. How do you deal with these things? God says run with endurance.

I remember a couple of years ago, I went on a 5K park run with a friend of mine. I hadn't been running for a while so I was a bit out of practice, but anyways …we decided to do the run together. About 1.5km into the race I felt like I was fighting to breathe, my mind was telling me that I couldn't do it anymore, that I should just quit; I don't have enough energy for this. This is what I call heartache in a metaphorical sense. As I started to slow down on my run, I was telling myself - and my friend who I was running with - that it was too much; I can't run for 5K; I'm going to quit – but she encouraged me and we kept on going.

Then on the second lap, now almost 3K into the race, it happened again – I felt like I couldn't breathe so I told my friend to go ahead without me and I'll meet her at the finish line - I actually just wanted to walk to the end in peace. But again, she wouldn't allow me to quit, she said that we can walk for 30 seconds then we need to run again. Every time I tried to stop running, she encouraged me to keep on going. So, after a couple more 30 second walks we kept on running – when we got to the last lap my friend told me that she was going to sprint just before the finish line, so I followed her and we didn't stop until we got to the end. I was so happy to have finished it; I looked back at all of the times that I wanted to quit.

That's how heartache - emotional pain or distress; sorrow; grief; anguish – can affect you.

Oftentimes, heartache makes you want to give up. Sometimes in the midst of painful and difficult situations, we can listen to the wrong voices or even start telling ourselves, "I can't do this anymore." But we can; God says run with endurance.

We have to keep on doing the things that we know are right even when we actually feel like giving up. Just as Jesus endured the cross, we also have to endure.

"You have not yet resisted to bloodshed, striving against sin."

Hebrews 12:4

The motions that I went through when trying to run the 5K race make me think of 'The Race of Faith.' This Christian race is a marathon! We're going to need endurance in order to finish this one. Things might happen along the way that cause us pain and heartache even to the point of wanting to quit but we have to keep on going. We might get to a point where we are literally fighting to breathe, it's ok to slow down, it's ok to catch your breath but it's never ok to quit.

On the penultimate lap of the 5K race, as we were going past the finish line my friend turned and said to me, "we definitely can't stop here." This was the area where all of the people who finished early and the park run organisers were standing by watching and cheering us on. It's harder to give up when you know that people are watching you – this is how we have to run this Race of Faith knowing that the Hosts of Heaven are watching over us and cheering us on:

"...since we are surrounded by so great a cloud of witness,' let us lay aside every weight, and the sin which so easily ensnares us, and let us run with endurance the race that is set before us..." **Hebrews 12: 1**

Endurance; the capacity to withstand an unpleasant or difficult process without giving way. Unpleasant and difficult processes on our Christian walk can be caused by many things such as fear, rejection, controversy and even offence.

This means that if we want to finish this race, we are going to have to display strength in the place of fear and confidence in the place of rejection; self-control in situations of provocation and forgiveness during times of offence. Ultimately, we're going to need to keep a right heart in order to see the plans and the promises of God come to full fruition.

"Lay aside every weight"

When God says lay aside every weight in Hebrews 12, what do you imagine? I imagine someone running a long race but carrying a large back packed full with heavy items inside of it. The person whom I see running is struggling to run upright; they are already tired from the distance but on top of that they are being weighed down by the heavy weight on their back. God wants us to lay aside every weight.

When I think of weights that have weighed me down during my Christian walk, I think of the weight of disappointment, the weight of anxiety and the weight of offence. These are weights that can slow us down on our race. Disappointment is a heavy ball and chain around your neck, anxiety is a broken clock and offence is a silent assassin.

In this message on perseverance God wants us to lay aside every weight.

<u>Physical weight</u>. The weight of disappointment will cause you to look down when you should be looking ahead. Think about it like this, when someone is disappointed it changes their whole countenance, it usually causes people to ask questions and wonder whether everything is ok with them. How do you picture a disappointed person? I imagine a disappointed person with their head hung down and most likely pondering on the situation that has disappointed them. Is this the correct posture to maintain when running a race? God wants us to lay aside every weight.

<u>Emotional weight</u>. Anxiety, the broken clock will either cause your mind to pause or it will cause your mind to race in the wrong direction. Anxiety is a feeling of unease, such as worry or fear, that can be mild or severe. Imagine a clock where the hands are constantly moving backwards in the wrong direction. Imagine trying to run a marathon, you're trying to focus on your breathing and pacing yourself along the path that lays ahead; instead, you have a million thoughts racing through your mind. This will slow you down, anxiety will slow you down, hence God says lay aside every weight.

[6] Be anxious for nothing, but in everything by prayer and supplication, with thanksgiving, let your requests be made known to God; [7] and the peace of God, which

surpasses all understanding, will guard your hearts and minds through Christ Jesus.
Philippians 4:6-7

Spiritual weight. Beware of the weight of offence; it has the capacity to slowly and silently cause you to drift away from the very people that God requires for you to be connected to. It won't always be obvious that this is happening, sometimes you may not even realise until it is too late. Offence, the silent assassin. He comes in subtly and buries his head beneath the bushes of a smiley face. Then he shoots stealth bullets when he thinks that no one is watching or everyone has forgotten about him. Sometimes in life we have to confront things head on, other times we just have to make peace within ourselves, forgive and let live! Sometimes you just have to step over people and let them deal with themselves.

If we are going to run this race with endurance then we cannot afford to carry around heavy weights.

The physical; the emotional or the spiritual, God says lay aside every weight and run with endurance.

The sin which so easily ensnares us
We also have to lay aside the sin that so easily ensnares us. To ensnare means to catch or trap something or someone like a spider ensnares a fly and other insect in its web. The Cambridge Dictionary also gives the following example:

"They wanted to make a formal complaint about their doctor, but ended up ensnared in the complexities of the legal system."

They set out to do one thing but ended up being caught up in another. Such is the way of the sin that so easily ensnares us. This is not the sin that we decide to turn our back on God and walk into, this is the sin that traps us whilst we are running our race for Christ. God says lay aside the sin that so easily ensnares you.

That sin could be different things for different people, it could be greed, anger, resentment, self-doubt, lack of faith.

What is the thing that usually tries to trip you up or slow you down on your walk? Do you find yourself constantly being tested in the same or similar situations in life? *Do you feel like every time you take a step forward you get pushed straight back to where you started?*

Perhaps you need to lay aside the sin that so easily ensnares you! These things come in all shapes and sizes but their aim is always to keep you from moving forward, to keep you from conquering and acquiring all that God has in store for your life.

In this message of perseverance, God wants us to run with endurance.

Mind Games?
One morning I woke up feeling annoyed and irritated by many different things that were being brought to my recollection. It was mainly to do with words that people have spoken to me – ever wish you could go back in time to a certain situation and answer that person differently? That's because the enemy wants to pull you back to a place that you have left! You don't need to go back and give an answer. God already answered them for you– sometimes God answers people with His actions.

"By awesome deeds in righteousness you will answer us."

Psalms 65:3

Now it's just noise, sometimes the devil wants to bring evil words to remembrance to keep us from moving forward. He wants to keep us from moving forward in our relationships, moving forward in our purpose and moving forward in our destiny.

That was the original plan, to kill, steal and destroy, remember?

John 10:10

Words are spiritual and can cause many emotions to rise up inside of a person. This is why evil words are one of the devil's greatest tools when trying to slow us down. The person that spoke the words may not physically be in your life anymore, it may be something that was said way back in the past. But evil words have an ability to bring back the same emotions of anger, rejection, inferiority or whatever else they caused the first time. The devil sometimes uses people to attack our character; our purpose and our destiny - they come in all different shapes and sizes. This is why we need the shield *and* the buckler.

You might be wondering, why? Why me? Well, the devil knows who to target, he doesn't come after those who are already his. He doesn't come after empty vessels either. He knows that there is a level of anointing on your life and if he allows you to reach your full potential you will pose too much of a threat to the plans of hell. Do not be deceived or ignorant, the devil knows your purpose even more that you know it yourself – he has watched you and clocked you and deemed you as a threat! Hence, he sends his assassins to target you with evil words, feelings of resentment, he's trying to cripple you with self- doubt and inferiority – anything that stops you from moving into your purpose. You need to fight back!

"His faithful promises are your shield and buckler."

Psalms 91:4

In this message on perseverance, God wants to equip us, we are going to need the shield and the buckler.

A shield is a large weapon of defence, it can be used to deflect attacks coming from afar – these are the obvious types, they come from strangers, acquaintances, maybe even work colleagues. Let's just call this the outer circle. You're going to need your shield.

But what about when the devil tries to use someone close to you, a friend, a family member or even someone in spiritual authority over you? What will you do when they start speaking evil words? They may not even know why they are attacking you but we know, the devil works through weak and wounded people – even Christians. They may have a crack.

Sometimes people can be going through things in their own lives where they are not on guard, that's when the devil uses them to cause destruction and confusion to those in close combat. Remember Judas! He may send them to you to speak words of discouragement. If you are not careful you will think that the person is your enemy and you will try to cut them off. You're going to need your buckler!

The buckler is a smaller version of the shield (up to 45cm in diameter) it can be used to deflect those attacks that come from people who are too close to home.

In this message on perseverance God wants to remind us of His faithful promises.

Ask God to protect you from spiritual attacks, ask for wisdom to use the shield AND the buckler. Resist the temptation to meditate on evil words and pray for the person that the devil is using. Remember we do not wrestle against flesh and blood! God is faithful and He is just, so meditate on His promises.

Psalms 91:10 *No evil shall befall you nor shall any plague come near your dwelling for He shall give His angels charge over you!*

When you go into a spiritual war you do not go in there alone.

"I will be an enemy to your enemies and I will oppose those who oppose you."

Exodus 22:23.

God takes it very seriously that the devil is trying to hinder you, it's a very dangerous position to be in when the creator of the universe opposes you! Sometimes you have to literally go to war over the things that belong to you.

"No weapon formed against you shall prosper..."

Isaiah 54:17

Message to My Maidservants

In this message on perseverance God wants us to run with endurance!

"I have given you the command to persevere that you may be my torchbearers, that you may be as light in the dark places."

God wants us to know that even in our darkest moments, or what we perceive to be dark moments, times of trouble, times of anxiety, times of depleting thoughts we must push through. God is watching us, He never left us in the dark times, He never left us in depression, He never left us in rejection or disappointment; He was cheering us on and is still waiting for us to get to the finish line.

Many things will come in our way to weigh us down or try to trip us up along the way. Don't stand behind that obstacle, step over it. Don't sit down inside of the dark tunnel, run through it. God has given us everything that we need in order to persevere in times of trials – James says count it all joy:

" ² My brethren, count it all joy when you fall into various trials, ³ knowing that the testing of your faith produces patience."
James 1:2-3

God has given us the tools to deal with anxiety and a recipe for offences. He has given us a way to overcome all the things that come to slow us down on our walks. God wants us to lay them aside and run with endurance.

Message #6 Run with Endurance!

Reflection & Prayer

Message to My Maidservants

Message #6 Run with Endurance!

Message #7
"Mother of Many Nations!"
A Message on Fruitfulness

For if these things are yours and abound, *you* will be neither barren nor unfruitful in the knowledge of our Lord Jesus Christ.

2 Peter 1:8

Many people when they hear the term 'fruitfulness,' they think of the Scripture in Genesis 1:28 where God says, *"Be fruitful and multiply."* Oftentimes people limit fruitfulness to the idea of getting married and having many children.

Let's look again at what God did in Genesis 2:

In Genesis 2:7, God formed man from the dust of the ground. He did this for a purpose. Then in Genesis 2:19, *"out of the ground God formed every beast of the field."* He did this for a purpose. God gave Adam the authority of naming every living creature, "And whatever Adam called each living creature, that was its name[2]."

---

[2] Genesis 2:19

However, in Genesis 2:22, *"the rib which the LORD God had taken from man He made into a woman, and He brought her to the man."*

Every living creature was formed from the ground, but Eve was created from the rib of Adam. There was something that God put inside of Eve that he didn't put inside of any of His other creations. Eve was the 'helper comparable to him.' Eve is symbolic of the first woman that God created. This means there is something that God put inside of woman, that he didn't put inside of any other of His other creations.

In Genesis 3:20, *"Adam called his wife's name Eve because she was the mother of all living."*

The Cambridge Dictionary defines the verb 'mother' as the act of treating someone with kindness and affection. To mother is a nurturing quality that extends beyond one's own biological children. Hence, Adam - by the authority of God - named Eve the mother of *all* living.

In this message on fruitfulness God wants you to know that you are a Mother of many Nations!

"Mother of many nations," - this is what God calls you!

Message #7 - Mother of Many Nations!
Her name is Angela, the year is 1980. Angela is eighteen years old and she is about to embark on a major life-changing journey. Motherhood. Angela has just had her first child – a daughter. Angela thought that she was destined to be a single mother but little did she know, God had a greater destiny for her.

Mother of many nations this is what God calls you.

"I met my daughter's father as a teenager, I was training as an athlete for a local sports club at the time. I must have been about seventeen years old when I met him. I wouldn't say that I fell in love with him, looking back now it was more like infatuation. By the time I was eighteen years old I was a single mum living with my mother and bringing up my daughter.

My dad had walked out and left us when I was about eight years old. That had a major impact on my self-worth; I always felt that he had walked away from me, that he didn't love me anymore. From that moment I felt rejection; that rejection I experienced as a child followed me into adulthood. From that point onwards I was seeking for love and fighting against rejection. I fought hard but that perception followed me into every relationship I had from that point.

Being a teenage mum was difficult to say the least, I couldn't do the things that my friends and other young people my age did. I felt as though I had two choices, either I hang around with other young people with kids or I stay around my family. The majority of the time I found myself gravitating more towards family. I had to find a healthy balance, as a child I knew what it was like growing up with a stigma of rejection. I didn't want my child to experience the same. It was enough that my daughter's father was not in her life, I was very careful not to let my daughter feel that same stench of rejection from me as a mother.

I also had to guard my own heart, I knew that there were things in myself that I had to work out and I didn't want to build any kind of dislike for my child as a result of it. Although I felt that aspects of my young adult years had been snatched from me, I knew that it wasn't my child's fault. I never wanted her to feel the burden of my mistakes. As a result, I was careful and deliberate about separating my relationship with my children's fathers from my relationship with them. I wanted my daughter's father to be more involved in her life, but I distinguished that he just didn't want the responsibility. I knew from then that I had to do it on my own and I had to be ok with that.

My Faith
My brothers and I used to go to church when we were little. Our mother didn't attend but we were picked up and taken to church in a van by the Pastor. My earliest memory of church is sitting under hours of preaching wishing I was someplace else. I remember being forced to go to church and then sitting under hours and hours of preaching with no revelation. It was a tedious and tiresome experience; I had no revelation of Christ. As my siblings and I started to get older we eventually reached a point where we had to make a decision. Were we going to stay or go? We didn't stay. After we stopped attending Sunday School and church services, I started to become very religious. My relationship with God was just reduced to: if I wanted something then I would pray. I knew that there was a God but I always thought that I would go back and serve God in my old years. By that I mean my eighties.

Being a Single Mother
After a number of years, I ended up getting into another relationship and having more children. This time I had two sons. I met my sons' father at college when I was twenty-two years old. At this point my daughter was about four years old. I was with my sons' father for a few years before we had our first child.

The year was 1990; I was twenty-seven years old when I had my first son. In 1992 I had my second son at age twenty-nine. I never chose well when it came to men. My sons' dad didn't get involved in my sons' lives when they were growing up. In fact, my relationship with him completely folded shortly after we had our second son. After I had my second son, I really had to think about my life, in particular my relationship with my sons' father. I knew that I had done it all wrong from the beginning in terms of having my children out of wedlock. But I also knew that I didn't have to continue down that road. My daughter was a major issue in my relationship with my sons' father. I didn't understand why that was such a major issue as he knew when he met me that I had a child from a previous relationship. I knew that it was down to me; I had to decide. So, I did.

It was 1992, months after my son was born, that's when I decided that enough was enough. I knew that I could not just continue to have lukewarm relationships where I ended up carrying the baby and the fathers were not sticking around for whatever reason. I have no regrets about having any of my children; I just didn't want to end up a single mum with a whole football team of children! Looking back now it's clear to me that these relationships were not going to work, our foundation wasn't right – it was just lust and emotion. So, after doing some serious self-searching I had a conversation with my sons' father and we parted our ways. I had to do it. I was not going to stay in a dead-end relationship. I had to go. It may seem like I was making a brave and bold decision but, in all honesty, it was one of necessity. I could just see where my life was headed if I stayed where I was. I could see it so clearly. I didn't see any point in having to sit down and explain my worth to a man. I didn't see any point in sitting down explaining why I should be engaged or why I should be married. I just didn't have the energy to sit down and explain my self-worth. I always knew deep down that something wasn't right.

Self-worth is a deep-rooted tree, but it won't allow you to rest beneath the shade of its branches. You have to sit on top, either that or you completely uproot it. Something in me ignited during that conversation and my sense of self-worth pushed through me. I knew what I had to do. I had to bring up these three children on my own.

I didn't like being a single parent but I just got on with life. After I had the boys, I decided that three children were enough for me to bring up on my own. I found it difficult. I didn't like the fact that I had to be both male and female in the relationship. Some days were easier than others.

At my lowest points I would cry out to God with my religious zeal and say, "God, get me through this!" I knew that there was a God, but at that point I didn't understand what it meant to have a personal relationship with him.

Breaking Free from Rejection

Eventually, I realised that it was up to me to make a difference, not just for my own sake but for the sake of my children as well. I had to look within; deal with the pain and break the cycle of rejection that had taken root inside of my life. I had to say no more, because I realised that I had a part to play in all of this and just agreeing to be hurt was something that I myself could control. For the sake of my health and the well-being of my children I had to do something. I also had to break free from the quilt of denial because I know that you cannot build a solid framework on a foundation of rejection. In that sense, I had to go back in order to truly move forward. I knew that I had to find my dad and find out why he didn't love me.

So, when my youngest son was eighteen months old, I travelled to Jamaica with all of my children. It was my first visit to the island; I went there to find my father. When I saw my father, the pain stopped. I wanted to tell him that I was sorry and that I didn't hate him; instead, he apologised and told us how much he loved us and that he had wanted to tell us that for years. My father told me that he was sorry for all the pain that he had caused. What was ironic was that the day I landed back in England I learned that he had died from malaria. I found him just in time. God allowed that burden to be lifted, had I not seen my father I would have believed that it was all of my fault. It wasn't. God wants us to be free from the pain of rejection.

I believe that it is important to understand how and why certain cycles begin in our lives rather than just focusing on the individuals who become entangled. In all honesty there could have been different individuals that I formed relationships with and the outcomes could have either been the same or different. It was just my choices at the time.

The Man Christ Jesus
I only started to see noticeable changes in my life when I came to Christ. The year was 2005, it was more than ten years since I had split from my sons' father. I met someone else. This man was no different, he had no interest in the things of God. Months after that relationship ended, I came to Christ. I knew at that point that if I was still in that relationship then I wouldn't have gotten to know Jesus.

I still remember the year that I got saved. It was like I was being pursued by God. Three distinct things happened in a matter of months. Firstly, there was a work colleague who asked me if I knew God; not long after that I met a woman on the bus who told me that Jesus loves me; then on two occasions, whilst walking through Lewisham I was handed flyers to come to church.

Although it was my younger sister that actually invited me to church at the Potters House; what made me step through the doors was my daughter. At the time I thought that my daughter was going mad. Her behaviour had changed so drastically. She would come home and tell me all about her new church and the sermons that she had been listening to. That wasn't too bad. However, she would also leave home really early in the morning with her baby to go to morning prayer. The final straw was when I heard that she had been preaching on the bus! I couldn't believe it. That was when I decided that I had to go down to the church and find out what was happening to my daughter.

Before I became a born-again Christian I always used to pray for my daughter. I prayed for all of my children but in particular I prayed for my daughter because I didn't want her to go through what I went through as a single parent. I prayed for my boys too. I prayed that they would not be like their dads - growing up and not having an input in their children's lives. Sometimes life is so subtle that you wake up and find yourself walking through doors that you once prayed would open.

I still remember one of my first encounters at my daughter's church, she introduced me to two sisters who later on became my closest friends. Although I went there to check up on my daughter, I attended the church for a number of weeks. Eventually made a decision to accept Christ. Once I made that decision to give my life to Christ, everything just made so much sense. I remember the sermon that was preached the day that I got saved. We had a visiting Pastor and he was preaching a sermon about being part of a union. I remember the words he spoke and it was as if he was speaking directly to me.

"There's someone in here ... God has a jigsaw puzzle; life is a jigsaw puzzle and He has one more piece that He needs to place and that's you. He's talking to you."

As the pastor continued saying *"you are the missing piece today,"* I felt that God was speaking directly to me. At this point I was crying and sitting up in my chair. Then the pastor gave an invitation to anyone who wanted to come and pray. I went up to the altar and I prayed. That day I invited Jesus into my heart; I haven't looked back since that day. I went all out and served God.

Raising Children as a Christian

I knew that I just had to let go and let God. After going to church for a few weeks and eventually months, I just felt peace and joy. I was in service and I had a thought. At the time I felt that the devil was taunting me:

"If this salvation is so wonderful and joyful then why aren't the boys in church? If this is so great then where are the boys?"

I came home that night and I said to them that they are coming to church with me on Sunday. There was a little protest at first but not too much avail because I had already made up my mind. They boys were getting older, they were teenagers, I didn't like the fact that they were out there on the street and not in church. After that day they attended church with me a few times. I didn't expect much. That was mainly because I thought back to my childhood days of being *told* to go to church. I just didn't expect this method to impact them that much. However, this time it was different. I distinctly heard the voice of God saying to me, *"I save."* That's where I got that peace from, my whole idea in bringing the boys to church was that I wanted them to be saved. That Word gave me peace.

Then, to my amazement on 28 August 2005, both of my sons made the best decisions of their lives, they prayed on the altar to receive Christ. My eldest son was fifteen and the youngest thirteen. God really did a quick work in mine and my children's lives. My sons; my mum and I all got baptised on the same day 1st April 2006.

My daughter got married in November 2007. My first son got married a few years later in May 2010 and my youngest son got married in June 2011.

God answered my prayers. As a single mother I always prayed for decent role models in my children's lives. My older brother helped out with the boys growing up, when they came to Christ, they also had Pastors and older men in the church that they could look up to. My younger sister was also a very influential person in all of our lives. God blessed us with such a supportive family.

Add to your Faith Virtue, to Virtue …
Throughout school I always took an interest in my children's lives. I was very visible and definitely had an input. Whether it was attending school functions or just telling them that they needed to have a purpose I was always talking to them and encouraging them to strive for excellence. I sent my sons to Taekwondo lessons because I wanted them to be able to hold their own. I would speak to them and tell them not to be followers but to be leaders of their own. I taught them not to give in to peer pressure. They didn't. When they came home with their friends, I would tell them their friends the same and encourage them all to behave themselves. As

a mother I would try and find out as much as possible about what was going on with them. Although I knew they wouldn't tell me everything, I would try. We're not given manuals as parents or as young brides; you just have to work things out through trial and error. I wouldn't say that I was perfect but I still had enough of a hold over my sons' that they would listen to me.

As a Christian mum I transferred my moral standards to my children. We prayed together; they watched me pray and they watched me praise God. My adult sons have a high level of respect for women. I believe that this value came from me praying and telling them that they must treat women in a certain way. Even at school I would instill in them that they should not fight girls. I always told my sons to look out for their sister – even though she was older than them. I also told my daughter to look out for them.

...Knowledge

As I grew in the knowledge of Jesus (2 Peter 1:5), I developed my ability to share Him; I began to know who God was. I began to meditate on Scripture and I realised that, "*the weapons of our warfare are not] carnal but mighty in God for pulling down strongholds, [5] casting down arguments and every high thing that exalts itself against the knowledge of God.*" (2 Corinthians 10:4 -5)

That is the knowledge that we need in order to understand that it is not by power and it is not by might. It is through Christ alone that a person can be saved and it is through Christ alone that a person can remain saved. Christ says that He will "*never leave us nor forsake us.*"

Hebrews 13:5

That means that He is going to go through the salvation experience with us. I began to realise that I can do all things through Christ who strengthens me. God helped me early on in my salvation. He gave me three Scriptures:

- "My grace is sufficient for you…" 2 Corinthians 12:9

- "For I know the thoughts that I think toward you, says the Lord, thoughts of peace and not of evil, to give you a future and a hope." Jeremiah 29:11

- "Be anxious for nothing, but in everything by prayer and supplication, with thanksgiving, let your requests be made known to God." Philippians 4:6

God gives us the Grace to serve Him, I realise now that God gave me the Grace to serve him. He gave me that assurance at the beginning of my salvation that His Grace is sufficient for me. I know that I can live for Him and that I can serve others because Christ – with the Holy Spirit – is the one helping me to live a life as a Christian. Now I understand what God meant when He gave me that Word.

Furthermore, the things that God has added unto my life, those listed in 2 Peter 1 v 5-7, I see now that those are God's Graces.

"…add to your faith virtue, to virtue knowledge, ^{6} to knowledge self-control, to self-control, perseverance, to perseverance godliness, ^{7} to godliness brotherly kindness, and to brotherly kindness, love."

You have to pray and have faith in God that He can do these things for you. He can do these things through you. You cannot live this Christian life in your own strength. Man will disappoint at some point but God will never disappoint. God will never leave you. You have to have that strength to keep pushing through even when people are laughing and mocking. You have to pray when trials come otherwise the devil will have you out there doubting and asking, why me? Be angry and sin not because God says that He has added perseverance. Through trials you realise what Grace God has imparted in you. Although the trials are difficult, you learn through them.

Perseverance through trials

My greatest trial came in 2017 when my younger sister died of cancer. In fact, that trial alone could have taken my whole family out. But again, God reminded me that His Grace was sufficient and that I was to be anxious for nothing. God gave me the grace to persevere. I remember asking God, why? I wanted to know why all of this was happening. I wanted answers. God said that He would give me peace. Oftentimes when trials come, we want healing; instead, God gave me peace for the hereafter. In this sense perseverance intertwined with the Grace of Godliness. Throughout this trial I had to seek God, it was the only way. God wants us to seek Him because He wants to give us that peace. I had to take the burdens off of myself and give them to God so that I could be free. Through my trials I learnt that you can always take your eyes off of your trials and help others, even if it's through prayer. I had to take my eyes off of the fact that my youngest sister was gone; I had to take my eyes off of the loss and realise that she is saved and has gone to be with Jesus. It took me a long time to get the peace that God offered me. That's because I was focused on the why instead of the now. I have to tell myself that my sister is at peace now. She is out of her pain.

The trials took a turn for the worse that year. In the same year that my sister passed away I was diagnosed with breast cancer. In fact, I had my operation the day that my sister died. When I first heard the news, I became anxious and nervous about what was going to happen to me. However, at my first consultation the Dr said to me, "*your story is not your sister's story.*" It was bittersweet. If this meant that I was going to survive my cancer diagnoses, it also served as a reminder of my sister's impending departure.

I remember the consultant's words, "*God would say your sickness is not unto death.*"

I believe that God was speaking to me through that Consultant. It was difficult for me to hear all of this, yes, I was being told that I would recover but at the same time my sister was dying. The why questions crept in again. It was particularly hard because I could *see* my sister dying. I had no choice at that point but to hold on to God's Word and pray for Him to give me peace.

Godliness. I had to know that I could hear from God. It was the only way. Over the years I had developed a habit of praying and getting peace, from this I knew when I had heard from God. During this season, I had to pray **Philippians 4:6** on a daily basis. I put God in remembrance of His Word when I said, "be anxious for nothing." God told me in the midst of my trials that He knows the thoughts that He thinks towards me and that He wants to give me peace. I realised that those same Scriptures that God gave me at the beginning of my salvation had come to life.

Even after I had been through the battle with cancer and was on my road to recovering, I didn't want people to know about it. I didn't like to talk about it. Looking back now, it's clear to me that the reason I didn't want to talk about it is because I was in denial. I felt as though if I didn't mention it, I could pretend as if it never happened. I felt this way for a while. Denial. This was a familiar place. I had been here before and I knew that it wouldn't work. You have to deal with things in order to get peace, you have to push through the pain. It's difficult but you have to do it.

In February 2020, my youngest son mentioned my battle with cancer in a sermon. I didn't know he was going to. It was the Grace of God that my son didn't run this by me first because if I had known then I would have told him not to mention it. So many people came up to me after the sermon as they didn't know that I had been diagnosed and recovered from cancer. Although a couple of people approached me, even more people approached my son and thanked him for the sermon. In that moment, God showed me that what I had been through was a message of hope for others. It wasn't about me. Brotherly kindness.

In the sermon my son shared his feelings and God showed me that my testimony is linked with the testimony of my family – for this reason I needed to make peace with it. My family is able to deal with things through talking, preaching or even through song. I had to put myself to one side. It is inevitable that my testimony will be shared at times by them because it is their testimony too.

I soon came to understand that the battle is the Lord's; I can do all things through Christ."

Message to My Maidservants

God wants us to know that His Grace is sufficient for us. Through our prayers we can do all things, we can even break generational curses.

Sometimes we may feel unqualified or inadequate to do the things that God wants us to do. In this message on fruitfulness, God wants us to know that our prayers are far reaching. He doesn't call us from the platform; He calls us from the pit. In that place of hopelessness when you think that you have nothing left to give. God calls you. Even in what seem to be the most unfruitful times of your life, God says: You are fruitful!

Mother of many nations, this is what God calls you.

We know by **Romans 4:17** that God calls the things that be not as if they are:

"As it is written, I have made thee a father of many nations, before him whom he believed, even God, who ...calleth those things which be not as though they were."

Abraham, by faith, believed the things that He was told and as a result He indeed became the father of many nations. God would say to us today that if we can believe in the things that we are told, if we could just begin to see ourselves as God sees us then we can indeed acquire the richness of his abundance. We can be all that He has called us to be.

2 Peter 1:5-8 talks about fruitful growth in the faith:

"...add to your faith virtue, to virtue knowledge, [6] to knowledge self-control, to self-control, perseverance, to

perseverance godliness, ⁷ to godliness brotherly kindness, and to brotherly kindness, love."

God says that if *these* things are yours, you shall neither be barren nor unfruitful in the knowledge of our Lord Jesus Christ. The word' *"barren"* has connotations of a womb that is unable to bear children. God says that if these things are yours then you shall be able to bear many children – mother of many nations. God wants your life to bear much fruit.

That's why He calls you who you are - Mother of many nations!

Message #7 Mother of Many Nations!

Reflection & Prayer

Message to My Maidservants

Message #7 Mother of Many Nations!

Message #8
"No Eye Hath Seen"
A Message on Abundance

"The thief does not come except to steal, and to kill, and to destroy. I have come that they may have life, and that they may have it more abundantly."

John 10:10

God promises us an abundant life. Have you ever sat down and wondered - What is this abundant life that God promises us? What does it entail? What does it involve? Are we living the life that Jesus died for us to live?

Abundance is a noun, the Cambridge dictionary defines it as, 'the situation in which there is more than enough of something.' As God wants us to have life 'more abundantly,' this suggests that He wants us to live a life in which there is more than enough of something. But what does this mean, more than enough of what? Most people when they hear about the abundant life, they equate it with material wealth and gain. Don't get me wrong, it is not the will of God for you to be broke.

Throughout Scripture, God gives many promises of his readiness to bless:

"The LORD will open to you His good treasure, the heavens, to give the rain to your land in its season, and to bless all the work of your hand. You shall lend to many nations, but you shall not borrow."

Deuteronomy 28:12

But is material wealth all that Jesus meant when He said He came that we may have life and life more abundantly? We know that there must be more to it than this because 2 Corinthians 9:8 tells us that:

God is able to bless you abundantly, so that in all things at all times, having all that you need, you will abound in every good work.

The adjective "all" has been repeated three times in this Scripture, therefore emphasising that the abundant life applies to every area of our lives. God wants us to abound (have more than enough) in every area of our lives. That we may live the life that God desires for us to have.

Message #8 - No eye hath seen

In this message on abundance, God wants us to go after our 'impossible' dreams! The bible says that dreams come from a multitude of a man's business (Ecclesiastes 5:3) but let us also remember that some dreams come from God. If we really want to live the abundant life that God wants us to live, if we really want to 'abound in every good work,' then we must enter boldly into the realm of impossibilities because that's where God is.

Five Keys to Living the Abundant Life:

1. **Seek First the Kingdom:**

The first key on the pathway to abundant life is to put God's Kingdom first.

If we really want to live the abundant life that God has for us, this will not be achieved by us going after what we perceive to be the things that bring worldly satisfaction e.g., popularity and financial wealth. The abundant life is a promise of God, and God's instruction is that we seek first His Kingdom. In seeking first, the kingdom of God He promises to add all other things onto us.

But seek first the kingdom of God and His righteousness, and all these things shall be added to you.
Matthew 6:33

There is an order to God's abundance, that order requires us to put the kingdom first. We are told not to seek after material wealth or worry about how we will clothe and feed ourselves.

Matthew 6:31 tells us, *"Therefore do not worry, saying, 'What shall we eat?' or 'What shall we drink?' or 'What shall we wear?"*

Instead, we are instructed to seek first the kingdom of God and rest in the promise that all these things shall be added to us. Let us remember to posture ourselves correctly before God, doing things in the order that is required of us.

2. **Trust God in all Seasons:**

What does this abundant life really consist of? God promises us that we will have all that we need – in fact He promises that we will have more than enough.

And my God shall supply all your needs according to His riches in glory by Christ Jesus.
Philippians 4:19

This does not mean that we should measure our lives according to monetary value because Luke 12:15 tells us, *"one's life does not consist in the abundance of the things he possesses."*

God promises to supply us with all we need, "according to His riches and glory." Therefore, abundance must relate to more than just riches and prosperity. The 'more than enough,' that God promises us encompasses the ability to have joy in all seasons regardless of our financial status. God can bless us with riches but He also makes it clear that we are not to trust in riches.

Paul tells us in Philippians 4:12, *"I know how to be abased, and I know how to abound. Everywhere and in all things, I have learned both to be full and to be hungry, both to abound and to suffer need."*

Here, Paul is telling us that he knows how to be brought low and he knows what it is like to have more than enough. In other words, he knows what it is like to have temporary financial setbacks and to have an overflow of goods.

In the following verse Paul tells us, "I can do all things through Christ who strengthens me."
Philippians 4:13

From this we know that the abundant life that Christ promises us is one in which He is able to sustain us through all types of situations and circumstances. If the economy were to collapse today, we can rest in the assurance that God will sustain us. We are not to put our trust in riches but in an all - encompassing God. The promise of 'life more abundantly,' is about more than just a promise to overload us with material wealth. We are not to hope for riches or trust them to bring us financial security, we are to put our hope in God alone to make provision for us in all circumstances.

"Command those who are rich in this present age not to be haughty, nor to trust in uncertain riches but in the living God, who gives us richly all things to enjoy."

1 Timothy 6:7

God's Abundance is a promise to give us everything we need to sustain ourselves in joy and purpose.

3. **Give Generously:**

There is a law of reciprocity when it comes to abundance. Reciprocity is a noun meaning the practice of exchanging things with others for mutual benefit. Jesus demonstrated a prime example of the law of reciprocity, He exchanged His blood for our sin that we may have abundant life in Him.

Jesus tells us, *"I have come that they may have life, and that they may have it more abundantly."*

John 10:10

'Abundant,' meaning a life that is more than enough; extraordinary; from the beginning of time God wanted us to be joyful and prosperous. Here, Jesus declares His intent to restore what was lost and bring mankind back to the state that God intended – the abundant life.

In order to access the full benefit of the abundant life, we are instructed to sew. Oftentimes people just expect to do nothing and get everything; God commands us otherwise.

38 Give, and it will be given to you: good measure, pressed down, shaken together, and running over will be put into your bosom. For with the same measure that you use, it will be measured back to you."

Luke 6:38

This imperative verb 'give,' could be in relation to time, money, talent, possessions. In this message of abundance, we are reminded of the need to sew generously into the kingdom of God. God has given us many things, for some it may be multiple gifts; talents and abilities; for others it may be material wealth and possessions, but we are commanded to give those things and in return it will be given to us, 'good measure, pressed down, shaken together.'

The verb phrase, 'pressed down,' creates imagery of a container that is filled beyond the top and so the goods inside must be suppressed to fit them inside and close the lid on top. This suggests that the amount returned will be more than that which was given as the amount returned must be pressed down to fit comfortably within the container. From this we can infer that God has a desire to bless us. God promises that in the same measure we give we will be given back and more so. The phrase *"running over,"* is a direct reference to abundance. We must sew into the kingdom; sew into the lives of others and sew into our dreams – this is the key to unlocking the door to the abundant life that God wants for us.

The law of reciprocity is not to be confused with the idea that we are simply giving so that we can receive. With all things pertaining to the kingdom of God, the law of reciprocity is about our heart posture. When we give, we are doing so in obedience to God and not simply because we want something in return. But we know that God is a rewarder of the faithful - **Hebrews 11:6**.

The secret of abundance has to start with us, Jesus gave His life, but we must *accept* His sacrifice in order to receive eternal life

– For *"whoever calls on the name of the LORD shall be saved."*

Romans 10:13

That is the same way we must continue to walk in obedience and trust in God that He will reward us with His abundance.

God says in **Malachi 3:10,** *"Bring all the tithes into the storehouse, That there may be food in My house, And try Me now in this."*

God is giving us a command to *"bring,"* but in the same sentence He invites us to *"try"* Him. Here God is demonstrating the law of reciprocity for in the following lines of the verse He says:

"If I will not open for you the windows of heaven And pour out for you *such* blessing
That there will not be room enough to receive it."

Here, God invites us to give generously out of an obedient heart and in return we will reap a harvest that is more than sufficient. He is a rewarder of the faithful.

4. **Maintain Perspective:**

God has given us strategies to manoeuvre through situations in life, there are certain things that we may have to go through if we want to truly experience all that God has for us. There are times in life where I have had to endure pain and hardship; I persevered only to find that I was going to reap a harvest at the end of it. There are times where God may position us in places and situations where we are called to deal with difficult people; people who have mistreated us or committed some sort of wrongdoing that seems to be going unnoticed. God gives us a strategy for dealing with these situations when He shows us how to treat our 'enemies'.

"But I say to you, love your enemies, bless those who curse you, do good to those who hate you, and pray for those who spitefully use you and persecute you."

Matthew 5:44

This Scripture is not to be misconstrued as to put us in a position of defeat, God tells us to love our enemies so that we can be more like Him, *"He causes His sun to rise on the evil and the good."* Loving our enemies and doing as God commands, leaves room for God to act on our behalf.

"By this I know that you are well pleased with me, because you do not allow my enemies to triumph over me."

Psalms 41:11

Sometimes God calls us to stay in seemingly uncomfortable situations surrounded by people who we may rightly perceive as "enemies." We have to maintain a right perspective because even in situations like this, God is setting us up to pour out His abundance. Our perception of abundance may just be a life where everything is smooth-sailing, and we are constantly being blessed by God without any resistance or restriction. But God promises us more than that and we must maintain a right perspective so that we do not miss out on the promises of God.

You prepare a table before me in the presence of my enemies; You anoint my head with oil; My cup runs over.

Psalms 23:5

The phrase at the end of the Scripture, *"My cup runs over,"* creates imagery of an overflow, a flood, an excess of God's goodness. This is a picture of God's abundance. This shows that if we manage to persevere and have a right perspective during the trials and difficult times of our lives, we are going to experience an outpouring.

The prepositional phrase, 'in the presence of my enemies,' means that the presence of difficulty does not negate the promise of God's blessing from flowing. It is all about perspective. We are not confined by our environment, our physical location or our circumstances; God promises to prepare a table even in the presence of our enemies. Sometimes we can be so busy looking left and right, look up because God wants to bless you.

Every good gift and every perfect gift is from above, and comes down from the Father of lights, with whom there is no variation or shadow of turning.

James 1:17

5. <u>Take the Limits off your mind:</u>

Now that we understand what is required to walk in abundance, let us take the limits off our minds and imagine big.

Sometimes our own limited perception of who God is could be the very thing preventing us from walking and living the abundant life that He requires for us. If we seek God with all we have, we will see that He is able to do exceptional things, great, unthinkable, and unimaginable things. Let us not just believe God for the ordinary but for the extraordinary because He is a God of miracles.

"Now to Him who is able to do exceedingly abundantly above all that we ask or think, according to the power that works in us,"

Ephesians 3:20

God is able to do way more than what we may ask or think, we think logically about what is within the confines of human capability, but God is able to do 'exceedingly abundantly above all that.' Let us pray in the Spirit and imagine beyond our circumstances because God moves according to the 'power that works in us.' This power being the power of the Holy Spirit.

Message to My Maidservants:
In this message of abundance God says, "Go after your 'impossible' dreams."

It is ok to want certain things for ourselves and for our lives, whether it be promotion at work; a nice house; the latest car; a financial blessing. However, when God speaks to us about the abundant life, He is talking about the extraordinary things that exist in Christ. These are immeasurable, indescribable, beyond our capability type things such as 'the peace of God that surpasses all understanding.'

Philippians 4:7

When we take the time to connect and draw close to God, He shows us things in the Spirit that may seem out of our reach to have and to obtain. Sometimes God calls us to do things that may seem 'impossible,' if we are looking at them through human eyes or relying on our own strength. But with God all things are possible. Those are the things that we must go after, because that's where God is. He is in the realm of impossibilities.

"The things which are impossible with men are possible with God."

Luke 18:27

In order to live the abundant life that God has for us, we must take the limits off our minds and walk according to the Spirit. *"For those who live according to the flesh set their minds on the things of the flesh, but those who live according to the Spirit, the things of the Spirit."* (Romans 8:5). When we bring our lives into alignment with the will of God, He will bring us into that abundant life where we have more than enough to fulfil every good work.

In this message on abundance, God wants us to go after our 'impossible' dreams, go after the things that no eye hath seen.

But as it is written:
"Eye has not seen, nor ear heard,
Nor have entered into the heart of man
The things which God has prepared for those who love Him."

2 Corinthians 2:9

Reflection & Prayer

Message #8 No Eye Hath Seen

Message to My Maidservants

Message #9
"For My Glory"
A Message on Purpose

For we are His workmanship, created in Christ Jesus for good works, which God prepared beforehand that we should walk in them.

Ephesians 2:10

'Purpose,' is a noun, it means the reason for which something is done or why something exists. European Law dictates that goods sold must be 'fit for purpose,' this means that the product sold is good enough to do the job that it was designed for. Manufacturers have to guarantee that goods sold are good enough to do the job that they are created for.

What does this mean to us? Our Manufacturer is God; He has a plan and a purpose for each of our lives. Purpose is the essential part of us, it is the reason why we were created. This is why we can never experience true fulfilment when we are not walking in our purpose. The only way to find true fulfilment is to do the very thing that God created us to do. What's my purpose?

Ultimately God created us to live for Him, and to worship Him; we were created for His glory.

"Everyone who is called by My name, Whom I have created for My glory; I have formed him, yes, I have made him."

Isaiah 43:7

In this message on purpose, God says "For My Glory."

Message #9 – For My Glory

Her name was Eve. She was the first woman ever created.

There was life in God's Garden, in a place called Eden. There God put a man called Adam. God gave Adam a purpose in the Garden, to tend to it and to look after it. Then the Lord decided that it was not good for Adam to be alone, so He decided to create a helper comparable to Him - **Genesis 2:18**. The use of the adjective *'comparable,'* has connotations of someone who is similar or complimentary to him. Furthermore, the use of the noun 'helper' suggests that God wanted to create someone who could *assist* Adam with his purpose in tending to the garden and looking after God's creations. So, God created Eve.

In **Genesis 2:21**, the Lord caused a deep sleep to fall on Adam, He took one of Adam's ribs and made it into a woman. Adam was astounded, and he said:

"This is now bone of my bones
And flesh of my flesh;
She shall be called Woman,
Because she was taken out of Man."

Genesis 2:23

Adam immediately recognised Eve as a part of himself, 'flesh of my flesh.' In the following verse God says, "For this reason a man shall leave his father and mother and be joined to his wife." The prepositional phrase, 'for this reason,' would imply that Eve's purpose was two- fold, she was created to help look after God's creation in the garden of Eden, however she was also created to be a wife to Adam. Adam called his wife's name Eve - **Genesis 3:20**.

However, when Eve was in the garden of Eden, she lost sight of her purpose! God created Eve from the rib of Adam; He called her to be a wife and a helper to Adam, but first and foremost Eve was created in the image of God. She was created for His Glory.

"So God created man in His own image; in the image of God, He created him; male and female He created them."
Genesis 1:27

Eve was one of God's image bearers on the earth. But she forgot her purpose. In Genesis 3 Eve started confiding in the serpent (the devil) talking about how God told them not to eat of the tree in the midst of the garden. The serpent struck up a conversation and Eve was drawn in.

"Has God indeed said, 'You shall not eat of every tree of the garden?" enquired the serpent.

"We may eat the fruit of the trees of the garden; but of the fruit of the tree which is in the midst of the garden, God has said 'You shall not eat it, nor shall you touch it, lest you die." The woman replied in gullibility.

"You will not surely die," replied the cunning serpent.

That was Eve's dialogue with the devil. But the real question is - Why was Eve talking to the devil? She was created in the image of God. For His Glory. Why was Eve sharing God's secrets with the devil? See Eve forgot her purpose! See now is not the time to be seeking counsel from the devil! Don't be like Eve, making moves with the serpent when you should be talking to God! Find your passion, pursue Christ and live out your purpose. Everything that He created has a purpose!

I created you for you to worship Me

In Genesis 3 v 6 we read that Eve ate of the forbidden fruit and then gave some to Adam to eat as well, she remembered to feed her husband! But she didn't seem to remember that she was created in the image of God, for His Glory. When God asked Eve what happened she replied in Genesis 3:13, "The serpent deceived me, and I ate." The serpent deceived her because she gave him a platform to speak.

Have you ever found yourself giving the devil a platform to speak? God had to banish Adam & Eve from the garden. See, Eve was talking to the devil instead of listening to God, when you do that, you lose sight of the reason why you were created. For His Glory.

My story

Before becoming a Christian, I didn't know who I was or whose I was, hence my life was quite disorientated. I was searching for purpose as opposed to walking in my purpose. I soon came to realise that:

"There are many plans in a man's heart, Nevertheless the LORD's purpose—that will stand."

Proverbs 19:21

My salvation experience has been a journey; I found myself when I found Christ. The more I got to know Him, the more I found out who I was in Him. God didn't reveal my purpose to me straight away. It was a journey of walking by faith; learning new things about myself; getting knocked down and getting right back up again. Scripture reveals that our overall purpose as Christians is to bring glory to God. Ask yourself this question, when God looks at your life do you make Him look good?

We were also given a great commission.

"Go therefore and make disciples of all the nations, baptizing them in the name of the Father and of the Son and of the Holy Spirit."
Matthew 28:19

However, there are some *specific* things that God wants us to do for Him. It is up to us to discover all of our gifts; talents and fulfil our purpose. There is a reason why each and every one of us were created in this particular time and season that we are living in right now. There is a reason why God gave us our individual gifts and talents. This is because there are things that God wants us to accomplish for Him on this earth. This is made evident in Ephesians 2:10 where God calls us, "His workmanship."

For we are his workmanship, created in Christ Jesus for good works, which God prepared beforehand, that we should walk in them.

The prepositional adverb "beforehand," means that prior to us coming to know Christ, God had already prepared works that He wanted us to complete. There is something inside human beings that searches for a reason to continue living. This is what makes us human beings.

What's my purpose?
Purpose is vital, it is the essential element as to why we were created. We are God's 'workmanship' and He has things that He has planned for us to do.

We need to take practical steps in finding out God's purpose for our lives – how exactly do we bring Glory to God in our individual lives. I am reminded of the parable of the talents in Matthew 25. The reality is that God has given each and every one of us different gifts and talents. You may have the gift of speaking; you may be able to speak words that change people's lives; use it for His glory. You may have the talent to sing, then sing people out of bondage, out of death, hell and the grave, use it for His glory. If your talent is writing – write for God. When you are pursuing your purpose, you will discover talents you didn't even know that you had.

Are you doing the very thing that God created you to do?

There is a strong interlink between destiny, purpose and calling.

Before I came to know Christ, I wanted to be an Actress and live in Hollywood. Acting was a passion that I had enjoyed as a hobby from a young age. Without God's direction I treated this hobby and talent as though it were my purpose in life. Although I realised early on in my salvation that moving to Hollywood to pursue my acting career was not my purpose in Christ, there were still other things that I was yet to discover about myself. I had to be open to the promptings of the Holy Spirit because God revealed things to me one blueprint at a time.

A woman's heart plans her way, But the Lord directs her steps.

Proverbs 16:9

I moved from New York City to London at the beginning of 2008. I started to immerse myself in the things of God by listening to sermons; getting involved in my local church and reading the bible. God took me on an inward journey as well as an outward journey. There were key scriptures that I meditated on during the early days of my salvation and they helped me to gain perspective.

For all that is in the world, the lust of the flesh, and the lust of the eyes, and the pride of life, is not of the Father, but is of the world.
1 John 2:16

As I read the Scriptures, I tried to draw distinctions between things that were 'of the world,' and things that were 'of the Father.' I got to know more about God through His Word. In my search I concluded that whilst pursuing the things that God laid upon my heart, I would find my purpose. I prayed and asked God for confirmation along the way.

It was the year 2009, by this time I had applied for and been awarded with a scholarship to attend Law School over here in England. I had to attend an interview; answer some legal problems and demonstrate my advocacy skills. It was quite an intense process but it all turned out to be worthwhile because I was awarded one of the highest scholarships that the Inn had to offer. This was enough for me to afford my Law School fees so I took it as confirmation that God still wanted me to be a Lawyer.

I graduated in 2010, and there began my journey of obtaining a pupillage - that is the 12-month stage of training that one must take in order to practice as a Barrister in England and Wales. I built up my experience as an Advocate by joining an Employment Law Charity, where I successfully represented clients in Employment Tribunal cases. I spent the next five years working in various law firms around London and trying to obtain my pupillage. Although I was not satisfied or fulfilled going from all of these different jobs with no clear direction, I told myself that it was only temporary as I was still applying for my pupillage. Being an Advocate for those who were unable to represent themselves did bring me a sense of fulfilment but going from job to job didn't. After a while I started to feel that there was something more that I should be doing. I was sure that I was destined to be a Lawyer, I searched for pupillages year after year. I kept getting close to these permanent roles but it never quite worked out. I was starting to get drained. Every time I wanted to give up, I reminded myself that I was doing what God wanted me to do and I kept going. I had friends around me that encouraged me to keep going because obtaining a pupillage was a difficult task.

In 2014, I made it to the final round of a pupillage application with a top Chambers in London on Bedford Row. At the initial stage I had to solve a legal problem before being invited to the final stage. At the final stage I sat through a rigorous process of tough questions being rotated at me by a team of Barristers. I had to be quick on my feet. This was the closest that I had gotten to my pupillage in almost five years. I thought that this was it. Out of a pool of three hundred plus applicants I was down to the last twelve. You can imagine my disappointment at receiving yet another rejection letter. Part of me was happy to have gotten so far in the process but the rest of me was just so disheartened. I asked for interview feedback and I was told it was difficult for them to provide meaningful feedback as I had gotten so far in the process.

They sent me an email with a part that said, *'I have no doubt that you have the ability to make it at the bar, and I wish you every success in the upcoming pupillage gateway application season.'*

Although it was a disappointing email to receive, I didn't give up straight away. I had a friend that encouraged me to keep on going and to continue being persistent. Part of me felt that I had done all that I could and if it still wasn't working then maybe God was redirecting me somewhere else.

By the end of 2015, I had enough of going from job to job and not walking in purpose. I decided that it was time to let go. I got relentless and decided that something had to change. This was about seven years into my salvation and I knew that there was more to my Christian life. I didn't expect everything in my Christian life to be easy but I believed that God had a plan and purpose for me:

For I know the thoughts that I think toward you, says the Lord, thoughts of peace and not of evil, to give you a future and a hope.
Jeremiah 29:11

I knew that it wasn't God's plan for me to be in an endless cycle. Although on the outside it seemed as though I had a goal and there was a purpose to what I was doing, that was no longer enough to maintain me through the low times. I had to look at my everyday life, how I was making an impact in this particular season that I was in. In between contracts I had to go to the Job Centre to sign on and I detested the feeling. It felt purposeless and brought a feeling of darkness over me. It wasn't life. I even remember my father telling me that I should go back to school and study something else. I had tried this Law career for about five years, something just wasn't quite working. God allowed me to find my own feet. Around the end of 2015 is when I had enough and decided to get radical about pursuing God's plans and purpose for my life. I didn't want to keep searching, I wanted to find and be found.

When I was in New York I was searching, I guess there were some aspects of my old mindset that still needed to be renewed. I was ready to let go. I prayed and I told God that if this wasn't what He wanted me to do then He should close every door and show me what He wanted me to do. I also made a decision not to go back to the Job Centre as God had confirmed to me through a prophetic word that I was to trust in Him for my provision.

"Why do you continue to doubt Me when I have proven myself to you time and time again?"

I asked God to reveal my purpose to me. I was ready to let go of all that did not align with God's will and purpose for my life. God, I'm giving you my dreams!! I gave my dreams to God and He re-wrote the script. From that leap of faith God took me to a new realm where I found myself on a whole new path. Towards the end of 2015 I was unable to get any contractual work in the law firms as before – this was the closed door that I prayed for. This was a quiet time of reflection for me.

At the beginning of 2016 I wrote down as one of my prayer requests, 'direction and stability in my career and finances.' I wrote it down in my journal and I wrote it on my prayer wall. In March 2016 God directed me to apply for a teaching job via a company called Teach First. I didn't get into the Teach First course but I discovered a new passion. Whilst preparing my lesson plan for the interview and assessment day I began to envision myself as an English Teacher. This was a time of transition for me. God stripped me from everything I relied on and knew about myself. 2016 was the year that I rediscovered my passion for Literature and I started writing a blog.

In March 2016 I ended up applying for a job as an English Teacher. This process started from an advert that popped up on my computer screen. This path was confirmed to me through a prophetic word that I received, "I see you back in school." This was the same year that I wrote my first book, Diaries of a Visionary – Inspiring Dreams. That's when it all came together. After I started working as an English Teacher, I was inspired to write two more books that cultivate the deep things of the Lord to the younger generation. I have been able to make an impact through my teaching and through my books. Although I found myself doing things that I never thought I would do, I found greater peace and fulfilment by walking in my purpose.

God has many more books that He wants me to write, and I will write them for His glory. I don't believe that any of my experiences in my salvation have been wasted, God can use everything we have at varying times and for different purposes. God opened a door for me to become a Lawyer and a Teacher and those doors have remained open until this day. At the beginning of 2021, schools were closed temporarily due to the Global Pandemic caused by Covid-19. During this time, God opened a door for me to work from home as an Attorney at a US Law firm. I hadn't worked in a law firm for five years. During this season, I came to realise that nothing I have been through shall be wasted. Eventually, God moved in a miraculous way and moved me to a school where a position was created specifically for me. When I experience difficult seasons in life, I am reminded of all that God has brought me through.

So long as we continue to walk in our purpose and do all that God has called us to do, He will cause all things to work together for our good. As I have become more accustomed to obeying the promptings of the Holy Spirit, I am able to discern when a season has expired. I am able to uproot myself with confidence and say, "What's next Lord?"

God doesn't give any of us a complete blueprint for our lives but these are a few key principles that we can live by when it comes to purpose:

1. Find a need and start to fill it;
2. Find your passion and pursue it;
3. Remember you are not just doing a job you are responding to a calling.

Calling is a summons that takes us to our purpose; purpose is the road that leads us to our destiny; destiny has a destination.

God called me to be a teacher but I had to realise that this was not my entire purpose. When I responded to the calling, I found myself writing books and being invited to speak at events. Purpose is found when we respond to our calling. We should bring this mentality to everything that we do. Finding God's purpose in every season of life is an ongoing reality for every one of us.

And we know that all things work together for good to those who love God, to those who are the called according to His purpose.

Romans 8:28

Message to my Maidservants:

Ultimately our purpose as women in the kingdom of God is to bring God glory. Just like Eve, we are God's image bearers on this earth. When people look at our lives, they should be able to see the Glory of God. As redeemed believers, we are a new creation in Christ. We are not just here, freed from sin and bondage but we also have a special purpose in Christ Jesus. God calls us "His workmanship."

For we are His workmanship, created in Christ Jesus for good works, which God prepared beforehand that we should walk in them.
Ephesians 2:10

Workmanship means the degree of skills and expertise that was put into making a particular product. You are God's workmanship. This means that you were hand-crafted by the Master craftsman. A great deal of skill and expertise was put into creating you, God's very own special work of art. You were created to carry out "good works." Although we are not saved by our works, we are saved for our works. Your skills and talents are unique, significant and were given to you by God. For His Glory.

Every good gift and every perfect gift is from above, and comes down from the Father of lights, with whom there is no variation or shadow of turning.
James 1:7

God gave us these individual gifts and talents so that He could use them for His glory. God wants us to put Him first. Thank the Lord for all that He has given you and ask Him to show you how to walk in your purpose; for this reason, you were made!

Purpose is the means by which God gets us to a place called Destiny. Calling is the summons that brings us into purpose. God's dream for your life is more rewarding and more fulfilling than anything you can ever dream up for yourself.

I created you for My glory.

Reflection & Prayer

Message #9 For My Glory

Message to My Maidservants

Message #10 "The Iron that Sharpens Her!" A Message on Friendship

---

As Iron sharpens Iron, so a man sharpens the countenance of his friend.

Proverbs 27:17

In this message on friendship God wants us to know that our relationships with other females are very important in the kingdom of God. He wants us to stand firm in the knowledge of who we are in Him; that our relationships with one another can reflect His glory. Therefore, be the iron that sharpens her.

Iron is a metal
The noun 'iron,' has two meanings. Firstly, Iron, is a metal - a brittle, hard substance, classified as a metal in Group 8 on the Periodic Table of the Elements. Iron is the most rich and plentiful of all metals. However, Iron is also an essential mineral that the body needs for growth and development.

"God says He wants our friendships to operate, "as iron sharpens iron…"

Proverbs 27:17

Oftentimes we may be in a place where we are looking for that "iron" when in actual fact God is calling us to be that iron. Notice that the Scripture says as "'iron sharpens iron." That requires two equally solid materials of the same nature that rub together in order to bring about great strength. As hard as it may seem, there are times when we cannot simply look for others to be that iron to us. Instead, we must in fact work on ourselves in order to become that iron that will be able to sharpen another.

Are you the type of friend that you desire to have? In this message on friendship God wants us to be…the iron that sharpens her.

Message #10 - The Iron that Sharpens Her

The year was 900 BC. Naomi lived in the land of Moab, there came a time where her husband and eventually her two sons passed away. Naomi and her two daughters- in- law were the only family members left in the land of Moab. Naomi left the land of Moab in order to return back to her home town of Judah, she told her two daughters-in-law to return to their mother's homes. They wanted to stay with Naomi but she ordered them away, saying that she had no more sons left to give them as husbands. Ruth means "female friend," and Ruth was a loyal female friend to Naomi.

The bible says that Orpah "kissed her mother-in-law, but Ruth, "clung to her."

Ruth 1:14

We don't read about what happened to Orpah after this point. However, in the following chapter Ruth says these words to Naomi:

"...wherever you go, I will go; And wherever you lodge, I will lodge; Your people shall be my people, And your God shall be my God."
Ruth 1:16

Some people don't even know how to comprehend what Ruth said to Naomi. Sometimes when same-sex relationships get a bit too close people don't know how to define it.

"Where you die, and there will I be buried."
Ruth 1:17

Although this may not have been her intention, through her loyalty and unbreakable bond with Naomi, Ruth ended up meeting her husband Boaz. This means that there was destiny attached to that relationship – Ruth and Naomie.

In Ruth 4:13 we learn that, "Boaz took Ruth and she became his wife." Eventually, Ruth bore a son for Boaz and she called his name *"Obed."* In Ruth 4:15, the bible says that Ruth to Naomi was "better--than seven sons." This is not a literal interpretation of the relationship between Ruth and Naomi, but this is evidence to the fact that relationships with other females are very important in the kingdom of God. Not only was Ruth's redemption assured through the relationship, but Naomie also received restoration and nourishment in her old age. Naomi took the child, Obed, and became a nurse to him (Ruth 4:16). Obed is the father of Jesse, the father of King David from whose line the Messiah-Redeemer would come. David was in the lineage of Christ. Therefore, there was destiny attached to the relationship between Ruth and Naomi.

God wants us to choose our relationships carefully; He attaches great importance to the relationships that we form with other females in the kingdom of God. In **Proverbs 12:26**, we are reminded again of the importance of choosing righteous friendships:

*"The righteous should choose his friends carefully,
For the way of the wicked leads them astray."*

I have been blessed to have faithful female friendships in my life and throughout my Christian walk. I remember a visiting Pastor came to preach at my church in May 2016 and he preached a sermon entitled, "Good friends save your life." I made some notes during this sermon, I wrote them in my journal and still refer back to them until this day. The Pastor broke a section of the message down into four categories which I am going to share with you in the section below. We all need these types of friends in our lives.

Friendship Goals: Which one are you?

- **The Comforter**: this is the woman who will help you focus and work things out. This is the woman who will stand side by side with you and pray with you through situations that you may be facing in life. The comforter will help you devise a strategic plan of action.

- **The Confronter**: this is the woman who is not going to enable you. When you are in the wrong in a situation or perhaps you are going down a self-destructive path, the confronter will stop you in your tracks and tell you what you *need* to hear in a spirit of love.

- **The Challenger:** this is the woman whose Godly life convicts you, even without words. Her faithfulness, her zeal, her passion for the things of God. Her Godly life challenges you to stand firm and go all out for Christ.

- **The Counsellor:** this is the woman who you can always count on to give you wise counsel; she opens her mouth with wisdom. When you ask for her opinion on spiritual matters, she responds diligently and with Godly counsel.

Let's pause for a moment and do some self-reflection. A healthy balance of these types of characteristics makes a mighty strong companion. The iron that sharpens her. Do we exhibit these qualities? Do we seek to surround ourselves with women who exhibit these qualities?

"He who walks with wise men will be wise, But the companion of fools will be destroyed."
Proverbs 13:20

God wants us to form Godly friendships with other women in the Kingdom of God. These are Divine Connections. Not only should we seek to surround ourselves with women that exhibit such characteristics, we should also seek to develop these characteristics within ourselves. The comforter, the confronter, the challenger and the counsellor – let us be the things unto others that we desire to have for ourselves.

"Let nothing be done through selfish ambition or conceit, but in lowliness of mind let each esteem others better than himself."
Philippians 2:3

God has not called us into a place of desperation. God has not called us into a place where we are at the end of a rope; willing to sabotage or sacrifice relationships with other females just to get what we think we want in life. This is not to say that Orpah did the wrong thing by abiding by her mother in-laws request for them to turn back. It is equally true to say that some relationships are seasonal, some relationships are circumstantial and some relationships last forever. Disappointment often comes when we take a seasonal or circumstantial relationship and mistakenly put it in the category of friendships that were built to last forever. Orpah may have had a seasonal relationship with Naomi, she had to know when her part in the story was over. Hence, Orpah kissed her mother-in-law and turned back. Ruth however, knew that her destiny was attached to Naomi – her forever friend.

"The Lord do so to me, and more also if anything but <u>death</u> parts you and me."

Ruth 1:17

That was a very bold statement for Ruth to make. From this we can deduce that Ruth was a prayerful woman, she knew that there was destiny attached to that relationship. She wouldn't let anything 'but death,' derail her from the will of God. Friendships are destiny related. Ruth was a loyal female friend to Naomi, later on in the story we see that she was indeed the iron that sharpened her and vice versa.

<u>Iron Sharpens...</u>
Swords, like many other sharp objects - knives, forks, surgical instruments - are made out of iron. Iron is a sharpening tool but has many other practical and necessary uses. For example, swords are used in battle, God wants us to be the kind of sharp iron that is effective in battle. Warriors with swords cause wounds.

Faithful wounds. Faithful wounds is an oxymoron, two contrasting words next to each other.
"Faithful are the wounds of a friend, But the kisses of an enemy are deceitful."
Proverbs 27:6

The juxtaposition within the Scripture, "faithful are the wounds," highlights the paradox that two seemingly contrasting ideas can co-exist in harmony. Faithfulness and wounding. Wounding has connotations of pain, suffering and physical bodily harm. On the other hand, the adjective 'faithful' means to be true, accurate and believable. Oftentimes, people take this Scripture and breed it out of context, this Scripture is not a call to go around pointing out the flaws that we may or may not notice in other women, thinking that we are just speaking truth. God has not called us to go around pointing out the flaws of others with no real purpose, intent or steps for redemption.

"She opens her mouth with wisdom, And on her tongue is the law of kindness."
Proverbs 31:26

Proverbs 27:6 is a call to loyalty. Loyalty in friendships oftentimes will require us to speak some harsh truth but God wants us to be the type of friend that causes wounds – faithful wounds.

It may not always be easy to rebuke people that we love, we often play the situation out in our minds wondering how they are going to take it. But God has called us to be that type of friend, that faithful friend – cherish the one who will tell you a harsh truth that hurts so much more than telling you a 'loving lie'.

"He who rebukes a man will find more favour afterward than he who flatters with the tongue."

Proverbs 28:23

Message to my Maidservants

It is obvious to us that meeting the right spouse will have an impact on our day-to-day lives and ultimately on our destiny. But, do we really comprehend the impact that our relationships with other females in the kingdom of God will have on that same destination. Your friendships with other females in the kingdom of God are unique, God orchestrated and God ordained. These are covenant relationships. A reason, a season or a lifetime. Therefore, be as iron.

As iron <u>sharpen</u>s iron, so a man sharpens the <u>countenance</u> of His friend.

Proverbs 27:17

A 'countenance' is an abstract noun referring to a person's face or facial expression. This is the image that we portray to the outside world – our countenance. Our countenance can also be impacted by internal factors, our thoughts and our emotions. In addition, the verb, 'sharpen,' means to improve, to refine or to perfect. This means that when one person 'sharpens' another's 'countenance,' they are causing that person to refine and perfect the way that they are presenting themselves to the outside world. Ultimately, they are helping one another to become better versions of themselves. Our friendships are meant to have this effect – making us better Christians.

Although some friendships break down because of disagreements, perhaps even words that were spoken, God's promises are real. If the words were spoken within the spirit of truth, then they may have caused wounds.

They may have caused pain, they may have even caused offence, but believe what God says because those wounds are faithful.

"So shall My word be that goes forth from My mouth; It shall not return to Me void, But it shall accomplish what I please, And it shall prosper in the thing for which I sent it."

Isaiah 55:11

May your faithful wounds continue to sharpen her even in your absence. God wants us to be that type of woman, the confronter, the comforter, the challenger and the counsellor.

As iron sharpens iron, so a woman sharpens the countenance of her friend.

Reflection & Prayer

Message #10 The Iron that Sharpens Her!

Message to My Maidservants

Message #11
"A Servants Answered Prayer"
A Message on Love

For your Maker *is* your husband, The Lord of hosts *is* His name; And your Redeemer *is* the Holy One of Israel; He is called the God of the whole earth.

Isaiah 54:5

In this message on love, God wants us to remember who we are. You are not just any woman.

Your Maker is your husband.

'Maker' is a noun used in the biblical sense to refer to God. Husband is not a native English word. It comes ultimately from the Old Norse word hūsbōndi, meaning "master of a house," which was borrowed into Old English as hūsbōnda. God wants us to remember that He is the Master of the house.

This is a message to the single woman as much as it is to the married woman. In a world where everything seems to be so inter-twined, being a single woman can seem difficult, almost like an anomaly. In seasons such as this God wants us to remember that He is the Master of our house. If you are reading this book from a place where you are already married then God wants you to remember who you are. His first love.

You are not just any woman; you are a servant's answered prayer.

Message #11 – A Servant's Answered Prayer
Her name is Pearl; the year is 2005 and she has just made the best decision of her life – giving it to Jesus Christ. Pearl didn't know who she was before she met Christ, but when she was eighteen years old, Jesus called her out of the darkness and into His marvellous light. God took Pearl on a journey, through a refining process and to a place where she was able to see herself just as God saw her. You are not just any woman – you are a servant's answered prayer.

"Growing up, I always thought that marriage was not for me. My parents separated when I was fifteen years old, this experience solidified those beliefs. It wasn't until I got a revelation of who Jesus Christ is that things started to change for me. In 2006 God changed my perspective on marriage. Throughout my salvation I began to understand marriage through living with various people.

In 2007 I lived with a Pastoral couple for over a year. During this time, I learnt about the importance of submission and the significance of having a man in the home. Not long afterwards, I lived with Uncle Danny and Sister Louise Robinson for three years between 2009 and 2011. This is where I learnt about the practicalities of married life, working as a team and how you allow someone to love you. I remember Uncle Danny taking Sister Louise on date nights. I also remember the way in which he spoke to and about her. He placed such high value on her as a woman. Living with them gave me first-hand experience of God's picture of marriage. Six years later I met my now husband, Rex; I was 30 years old by this time. During the years leading up to when I met my husband, I experienced some of the most difficult trials of my salvation to date.

My salvation journey was an inward journey. When I first got saved in 2005, I was able to let go of the outward things, for example I was no longer clubbing and listening to certain types of music. I filled my time with the things of God because I had a burning desire in my heart to do things for Him. I started travelling around the world, going on impact teams and getting involved in ministries at my local church.

Health Issues
In September 2010, five years into my salvation, I started to experience health issues. I had symptoms of Chronic Fatigue and Hypo Thyroid Amalgamation but no official diagnoses; I lost the ability to move. There were days when I couldn't really move my body at all; I was so tired that even phone conversations would drain me. I had to stop. That's when I realised that all of this time, throughout the years of my salvation I had just kept myself busy. I was trying to be a 'human doing' instead of a human being.

Between 2010 and 2015 I had no diagnoses in relation to my health so I continuously pushed myself, I continued travelling, visiting friends and going on various impact teams. I also travelled to our annual church conference in Tucson almost every year. I even started working twelve hour shifts at my job in order to fund myself. I worked as a Healthcare Assistant at Great Ormond

Street Hospital for four days a week. This was an even harder push.

Although travelling was starting to take its toll on my health, I continued to push myself. Travelling was my way of escape from reality, my way of showing myself that everything was normal. I enjoyed travelling and going on impact teams. I felt that if God was still opening doors for me to travel this meant that I was ok with Him. I went on two impact teams in 2010 –Sierra Leone and Gambia. We also stopped over in Kenya for a couple of days on our way from Sierra Leone, the excitement of being in another country gave me further assurance that God was pleased with me.

I knew back then that my salvation was going to be a faith journey because whilst on my way to Sierra Leone in March 2010, I was praying and God gave me a Scripture. I didn't know at the time exactly what this was related to but I knew that something was about to happen.

"For the vision is yet for an appointed time; But at the end it will speak, and it will not lie. Though it tarries, wait for it; Because it will surely come, it will not tarry... the just shall live by faith"

Habakkuk 2:3-4

I felt God telling me that although the vision will tarry, I should not lose heart and also that it is faith that is going to get me through the next season. I thought this was God's way of preparing me for something that was about to happen in Sierra Leone. Favour started from early on. I was travelling to Sierra Leone on a medical mission; I got stuck in traffic on the way to the airport and ended up missing my flight. I was travelling with a group of people. They had left on Wednesday and my flight was meant to be on Thursday but once I arrived, I was so late that there was no one at the check in desk! I ended up going back to the airport on Friday morning. God gave me favour once I got to the airport and the lady ended up giving me a new flight the following day for free. I believe that God orchestrated this to reveal to me a new level of His Sovereignty; I would need that for what was to come.

When I went to Gambia in September 2010, I fell sick with food poisoning. At this point I was reminded of the Scripture from Habakkuk and I believed that my health was going to get better soon. I hadn't yet grasped the fullness of my journey and how much my faith was about to be tested.

My journey continued.

In 2011 I started a new job as a Healthcare Assistant at Great Ormond Street, three weeks later my health significantly declined and I had to take months off of work. During this time, I had already booked to go to the Tucson conference but fell extremely sick just days before I was due to travel. I had many different symptoms, fatigue, gut imbalances, brain fog but no actual diagnoses. I was starting to have neurological symptoms that prevented me from walking. It progressed to the point where one morning I woke up and I just couldn't move. That's when I ended up in hospital.

Whilst I was in hospital God gave me a Scripture from Jeremiah 30:17: *"For I will restore health to you And heal you of your wounds..."*

I clung to this Scripture throughout my health journey and throughout the years of my salvation.

In 2012, I was still unwell but I went to visit family in Uganda because my grandfather had passed away. Whilst I was out in Uganda, I found that my health had significantly improved. At this point, I believed that being close to family was what had made me better. For a little while my health remained significantly better so I started doing more for myself and even went back to working full time at Great Ormond Street. I was astonished that they had kept this job for me, even though I had only worked there for three weeks before I fell sick. God gave me great favour because I received a pay cheque every month throughout the time that I was off. God would always remind me that He gave me that job and that He was the one sustaining me.

In 2013 I travelled to Los Angeles; Tucson; Turkey; and Israel. In November 2013, a week before I travelled to Turkey and Israel, I attended a conference in Walthamstow. God challenged me to give a certain amount of money into the offering. When I counted all of the money in my accounts it made up the exact amount that God had told me to give at the conference. So, I gave it all. I emptied out my pockets and went to Turkey and Israel with no money in my pockets. Once again God reminded me that He had made provision for me, at this point I was tired of living by faith I even began to despise it. Despite my own feelings, I got to see that there is nothing that God cannot do. I was on that trip for ten days and there was not one need that was not met plus more. I even came back with money that I didn't have when I went there.

In 2014 my health was strained internally – I knew that I wasn't 100% - but I suppressed my inner voice and decided to keep on going. I attended an impact team in

Ghana as well as travelling to Tucson, Los Angeles, Amsterdam, Singapore, Australia, France and Athens. God gave me favour with flights; He gave me such a grace for my travels. Although my health was struggling, I kept trying to push; I just wanted life to be normal again. I was pushing myself to travel to all of these places because I wanted to prove to God that I was ok; but God already knew what was going on and He prepared provision for me to rest. He showed me that I didn't need to prove anything to Him. I would go to places and people would just look after me. I knew that it was God setting me up. Although I couldn't communicate my struggles to God, He knew just what I needed.

By 2015 my health had taken a downward spiral. In March 2015, I cut down my working hours to one day per week. I struggled to make it to the Tucson conference but I also travelled to Los Angeles, Spain and Morocco. I enjoyed my time travelling as I got to learn about different cultures and people, but I found myself struggling to accept my reality. My health was deteriorating.

Chronic Fatigue Syndrome
In May 2015 I was diagnosed with Chronic Fatigue Syndrome. This was a diagnosis that I struggled to accept, I just thought it meant that I was tired. Reality soon hit me. Between 2015 and 2017 my health went from pushing myself to the limit to a place where I was unable to do anything at all.

I was literally stuck in my room. I lived in my room. I was stripped of everything that I was at that point. I couldn't travel, I couldn't go to impact teams. I read three chapters of Scripture a day asking myself, who am I? Eventually, my health got to a point where I could just about make one church service a week. That's when I reduced my working hours. During this time God was faithful, He kept sending people my way who were taking care of me. Throughout those two years God was carrying me and taking care of me. God was showing me that He didn't need me in order to get things done and also that He didn't condemn me for being sick. The Scripture from Jeremiah 30:17 came back and upheld me.

"For I will restore health to you and heal you of your wounds..."

I also began to meditate on **Psalms 27:14**:

Wait on the Lord; Be of good courage, And He shall strengthen your heart; Wait, I say, on the Lord!

That Scripture reminded me of the Scripture God gave me in Habakkuk in 2010, it was all coming together. In my mind I was thinking, "I haven't got time to be waiting," but I had no choice. I had to wait. Every time I tried to push myself, my leg would start aching. I had no mental energy; it would take me three hours to process a Scripture in my bible. I had no choice but to just wait and let God look after me.

In 2017, I received another diagnosis, this time it was for Hyperthyroid. The Doctor said to me, "You look like you're in a waiting game, be kind to yourself at this time; you just have to wait."

During that time, I also remembered a word that Evangelist Jerry Fussell gave me in 2015.

He said, "God is shaping you to become a woman of formidable prayer – coming from a place of solitude."

I had found myself in that place of solitude and all I could do was pray. The Scripture from Habakkuk came back to me again and I was reminded that the just shall live by faith.

God was showing me that the value in who I am wasn't based on what I did. I grew up thinking that my identity was found in the things I did for example whether or not I did well at school and got straight A's. I found myself constantly doing things to gain approval and win people's love. I had the wrong mindset, believing that God was only happy with me when I was doing things for Him. I needed to know that God's love was not based on the things I did but that God loves me because I am His child. God wanted me to know Him, His heart and not His hand. God wanted a relationship with me. This season of sickness gave me a right perspective, I realised who I was in God. I also began to realise that having this right perspective of who God is, was going to help me later on in marriage. I found that my value was in Christ.

These were the years of God forming that heart and mindset in me. I realise now that God put me in that place because He had to sift some beliefs that had formed in me. After salvation, there are things that rest in our subconscious. These are mindsets and thought patterns that are not of God. He has to break them; He is the Master of your house.

Your Maker is your husband, the Lord of Hosts is His name and your Redeemer is the Holy One of Israel.

Isaiah 54:5

Marriage?

By June 2017, I had given up on a lot of my hopes; I had been living in my room for two years. I had spent all of the money that I had. My reality and my faith were clashing. Hope was distant for me. I hoped that one day I would get married but I couldn't even comprehend how. I was sitting in my room, not in ministry and unable to go anywhere.

"How is anyone going to find me here?" I wondered.

Everything I enjoyed had been snatched away, I wasn't at my best and I felt that I had no hopes of meeting anyone.

In June 2017, a friend of mine messaged me from Canada saying that she had a friend that she wanted me to meet. She didn't know how sick I was so I told her that I would pray about it in order to get her off of my back. I didn't get back to her for two months. At the end of August, she messaged me again and I started praying against it saying "God get her off of my back." I wasn't in any position to meet anyone, I was not where I wanted to be spiritually, emotionally or financially. However, I believed that during this time God was telling me to just be open.

In September 2017 I managed to attend a healing crusade in Spain. The Pastor gave me a word. He said, "God wants to heal you but the words you keep speaking to yourself are damaging."

I had given up hope and it was showing through my words.

I remember saying, "God, you don't love me, You stripped me of everything and now you want to bring someone to come and see me like this."

Message #11 A Servant's Answered Prayer

I wasn't ready. A dear friend of mine, Sister Cheryl came from Jamaica to visit London in mid- September. I tried to get her on side by telling her that a friend of mine in Canada was trying to set me up with this guy. Then she said that I should just be open and see what God does. That was the second time I heard that I should just be open about this situation. My friend in Canada messaged me again to say that it would be good for myself and Rex to meet at the conference in London in October that year. I still wasn't feeling good about myself and was giving every reason as to why they couldn't come. About a week before the conference in London, God gave me a supernatural strength to get up and be active. So, I was able to attend the conference and eventually I got to meet Rex.

When I first met Rex, I decided that he definitely wasn't for me, he was too quiet, besides that he didn't look like he was my type. I never imagined my husband being Asian. Nevertheless, we had a few conversations and exchanged numbers before he left for Canada. I got to know him a bit better just by being open. Rex is very reserved so he was not giving off a lot about himself. By December 2017, God started to show me things in Rex that were things that I had prayed for. I wanted someone that had their own personal convictions; was driven by a revelation of what God had said and was solid in who they were. I'm a strong character and I needed someone who could match that character in me.

In March 2018, Rex asked me to come to Canada. I didn't have any money to travel but Rex offered to pay for my ticket. Although I hadn't been working for the past couple of years and didn't have much money, I told him that I didn't need him to buy me a ticket. God showed me that I was prideful. I did need him to buy my ticket because I couldn't afford to pay for it myself.

I wanted to show God that I was open so I went to Canada, when I got there, I was pleasantly surprised. In Canada I got to see Rex's heart. I was staying with a friend in Canada. One day, Rex came to our house with a bag of Jolly Ranchers; we had been looking for them the day before as I wanted to get them as a present for a friend of mine who had requested them. This day was Good Friday and not that many shops were open. I came to find out that Rex had driven everywhere, he made it his thing to go and look for the Jolly Ranchers that I wanted. That's what I mean when I say he showed me his heart. Rex was not much of a talker; I wouldn't describe him as charismatic but he is someone that shows love by his actions.

Rex ended the trip by telling me that he liked me and that he wanted to spend more time getting to know me. We decided that from April until June we would be intentional about getting to know each other. By this time, we were thirty-two and thirty-four years old so we didn't want to waste unnecessary time. I still wasn't completely healed from my health issues but I was trusting in God. When I got home I prayed and asked God to heal me once again. That's when God told me to, "Get rid of the wilderness mindset, it's time to go forward."

What did that mean? It meant that although I wasn't healed from my sickness, I had to move forward. The courtship with Rex was me going forward. I told Rex that I was dealing with some health issues; I kept praying; sought counsel and we moved forward.

The Courtship
I went back to Canada in June 2018. This time around I travelled down with some friends from London. That's when Rex asked me to be his girlfriend. He brought me flowers, decorated the garden with balloons and he wrote a heartfelt letter. I was overwhelmed. We dated for six months after that.

In December 2018 I went to Canada to meet Rex's family, that's when we got engaged. I was still suffering from the same illness but I was able to travel so long as I kept my activities to a minimum. Although I was constantly praying and believing in God for healing, I found that Rex was willing to take me on even in my sickness and he understood me. He knew that my life was going to affect his, but that was ok with him. Rex was so thoughtful and considerate; he would make plans but he would always reassure me that if I was not well enough to carry them out with him then that was ok. Rex would always cater to my needs; I look back at that season and I can take away so many things that God did for me.

Firstly, God gave me a long-distance relationship, this was great because it alleviated me of the pressure to entertain Rex with activities. I just didn't have the physical strength to do so. Secondly, I was not where I wanted to be within myself. I was not satisfied with where I was at in my career, my finances or my health. But God allowed that to happen in order to show me that Rex did not see me by my achievements, he saw me for who I was. Finally, I learnt that when God does things, it doesn't have to make sense; you just have to be ready.

Not long after Rex and I got engaged, I fell really sick. Between January and May 2019, I was practically in bed sick the whole time. I was due to leave England in August 2019 and move to Canada. I had no idea how it was going to happen. I was thinking that this was how I was going to finally get healed, just in time to move to Canada but God said no. God wanted me to know that He did this; He made this happen.

Whilst I was planning my wedding, I was weak and had very little left in terms of finances. I had no money to buy the wedding dress. I remember praying and asking God if it would be possible for my parents to cover the cost of my wedding dress. God replied "Am I not your Father in heaven?" I was very specific in my prayers, I told God how much I wanted to pay for a dress. God sent me onto Google. I followed the exact steps that were given to me. God showed up for me in miraculous ways. I remember getting the wedding dress of my dreams at just a fraction of the price; a lady that owned it decided to give it away for £100's when it was worth £1000's. God challenged me to ask for an even further discount. The lady took off another £100 or so. He orchestrated everything even down to the wedding day.

Rex and I got married in September 2019.

A Servants Answered Prayer
Rex got saved in 2001, he spent eighteen years in the same church before we got married. He said that he had been praying for a wife although not actively looking. After we got married Rex told me that he had always prayed for a woman that was extroverted, loved being around people and also had her own convictions. Since we have been married Rex continuously reminds me that he always prayed for someone like me and that he got blessed beyond measure. There are two women in Rex's church – two Pastors Wives – that have the qualities that Rex prayed for in a wife. These are the two women that people always tell me that I remind them

of. I didn't even know these women at the time when Rex was praying; I only met them once I moved to Canada. God did this.

When I didn't even know who I was, someone out there was praying for someone just like me.

Message to My Maidservants

Many times, we want God to write our love story but we have our own idea of what we think it should look like. Are we willing to relinquish our control when God's script doesn't look like the one we have written? Oftentimes it seems that we are so able to relinquish control in some areas of our lives more readily than others, we trust God with our souls but not with our spouses. God wants us to relinquish control and trust Him in every area of our lives.

He has designed it that, *"the just shall live by faith."*
Hebrews 10:38

Are you ready to dwell by faith in the land of promise?

Abraham demonstrated his faith by obedience, *"[s]he waited for the city which has foundations, whose builder and maker is God."*
Hebrews 11:10

God wants us to know that He has a special plan and a purpose for our lives. He has a love story that He has written for us that is intertwined with purpose.

Are you willing to wait for it?

Your love story is unique. Remember, you are not just any woman; you are a servant's answered prayer.

Reflection & Prayer

Message #11 A Servant's Answered Prayer

Message to My Maidservants

Message #12
"For Such a Time as This"
A Message on Destiny

For I know the thoughts that I think toward you, says the LORD, thoughts of peace and not of evil, to give you a future and a hope.

Jeremiah 29:11

God wants us to know that our role as women in the Kingdom of God has been preordained. Woman of destiny!

'Destiny,' is an abstract noun. The Cambridge dictionary defines it as "the particular state of a person or thing in the future, considered as resulting from earlier events." These 'earlier events,' could be different decisions that you have made in life, these decisions ultimately lead you to a particular state or place of being. That particular state or place of being is called Destiny. Destiny has a destination.

God wants us to know that we have a destiny in Him.

In the bible, Queen Esther was called into the kingdom during a time where the King had ordered all of the

Jews to be put to death. Esther was also a Jew, but she reasoned in her heart that she should not get involved because the King had already ordered that anyone who entered the king's inner court without being summoned should be put to death. Well, all except for the one who found favour in the king's sight. Esther wanted to keep silent, until Mordecai confronted her with this question:

Who knows whether you have come to the kingdom for such a time as this?
Esther 4:14

Message #12 - For Such a Time as This:
Her name is Norma; the year is 1981. Norma is eighteen years old, and she has just made the best decision of her life - surrendering it to Jesus Christ. God is about to take Norma on a journey from Faith to Destiny.
"Four months after I got saved, I started dating my now husband, Fred. We started dating in December 1981. At this point, I had just turned nineteen. Fred proposed to me in March of the following year, 1982. However, we weren't officially engaged until April 1982 after he had spoken to my father and asked for my hand. Fred and I were engaged for nine months; we got married in January 1983. I was 20 years old when I got married. We had our first child, a daughter, in August 1984.

At this time, Fred and I were attending The Door Church in Tucson Arizona under the ministry of Pastor Harold and Mona Warner. Whilst Fred and I were dating, he had told me that he was called to preach so I knew that he was going to be a Pastor one day. I prepared myself to be a pastor's wife. We became the Door Directors of the church in May 1985. This meant that we were Pastor Warner's right-hands. Anything that he needed help with in the day-to-day running of the church, he would call upon us. We were the Door Directors for one year. God used this time to prepare us for what was next. Things were moving so quickly for Fred and I, but I was ready for it.

Pioneering ...
Three years into our marriage, the journey began.
In 1986, at our May Bible Conference, Fred and I were sent out to take over a church from a couple in Laredo, Texas. The church had not been open for even a year the time we got there. As I knew years beforehand that my husband was called to preach, I was able to prepare my mind for the journey. I didn't know where or when we were going to be called upon but I knew that it was only a matter of time before we got sent out onto the mission field. The day had finally arrived, my emotions were in a whirlwind, both nervous and excited at the same time. I had surrendered my life to Jesus at a young age and was excited to see what God was going to do next.

First Stop Texas...
When we got to Texas, it was difficult to find work due to the state of the economy. Pastor Warner and the church were helping us with the rent of the church building. Fred managed to get a job to support us as well. However, during this time, the economy was starting to collapse. Many businesses were starting to close down and people were moving out of town to the next city, San Antonio. There was a military base in Laredo that had been moved, this also added to the increasing difficulty in finding jobs.

The couple that we took the church over from were struggling financially as well. So, at the next church conference in November 1986, Pastor Warner reviewed the situation in Laredo and saw that it wasn't getting better. There were a handful of people in the church (about five), and not enough employment to sustain us. Pastor Warner decided to close the church down and have the people go to another church in the area. We didn't spend long in Laredo, Texas. We were there for six months in total. This was our first taste of Pastoring a church.

Eventually, things got better in Laredo, Texas. Within a couple of years, the economy improved and Pastor Warner was able to send another couple out there to pioneer. However, I believe that God used the situation with the economy to move us on. It was God's timing. That same year an opportunity arose for us to take over a church in Las Vegas, New Mexico.

New Mexico

Following our church conference in November 1986 we left Texas and went to take over the church in Las Vegas, New Mexico.

We spent eleven years in New Mexico – it felt just like home. As the years went by, I grew even more attached to the church in New Mexico. My son was born there on 7 January 1988. I saw myself never leaving. New Mexico was home to me.

Our church stood in a small town of approximately 15,000 people. It was very family orientated and close-knit. There was a lot of poverty in our town in New Mexico. But it was such a beautiful experience to serve and build a church there. There were two Catholic churches and several Protestant churches with buildings. We were the second biggest church but we didn't have our own building.

We know that the Lord, "does not live in temples built by human hands."
Acts 17:24 (NIV)

However, my husband Fred is a visionary, he sees things that I don't always see. Not long after we moved to New Mexico, he felt so strongly that the church needed a building of its own. It was difficult to grasp because there was a lot of poverty in the church. The prospect of owning our own building just seemed so far-fetched. But Fred felt so strongly about this, he knew that having a church building that they could call their own, would give the people a sense of dignity.

We saw God perform miracles for us in New Mexico. We saw God build His church.

A dignified place to meet...

With the level of poverty that existed in that town, it was nothing short of a miracle that we were able to get a building. To put it bluntly, a vast majority of the people in New Mexico were unemployed, they were living on food stamps. In the UK we would call it Job Seekers Allowance. It looked like an impossible situation, there was nothing we could do. Fred and I began to pray and trust God. God moved upon the hearts of the people in New Mexico, they gave out of their poverty.

In 1988, Fred challenged the people to trust God for a whole year and not rely on the Government for money. When they stepped out in faith in their personal finances God gave the increase. After trusting God with their finances for a whole year 9 out of 10 people started getting jobs. The church stepped out in faith and we saw God move.

In 1990 my father-in-law lent us money to purchase a piece of land upon which to build. Once we had that land, we used it as collateral to take out a 30-year mortgage with the bank. We borrowed 300K from the bank and used the first 35K to pay Fred's dad back. We had the land; we had the mortgage and we saw God move.

The people in New Mexico, gave like the widow with two mites.

"for all these out of their abundance have put in offerings for God, but she out of her poverty put in all the livelihood that she had."

Luke 21:4

We started building that same year, 1990, at this point 90% of the congregation had jobs. God continued to bless them with homes and cars. The church started to grow.

Coming into my own...
I started up a women's bible study on Tuesdays. I shared a book about the women of the bible that were used by God. We started getting visitors and I asked a Pastor's wife from the local area to come down and be a guest speaker. Eventually our small group of five to six women developed into dozens and when we staged special events and luncheons more than a hundred would gather. We saw miracles stemming out of that prayer group in Las Vegas, New Mexico. Prayer requests were being answered. It was tremendous, especially when children started getting saved. Teenagers as young as thirteen were being radically saved just by their mother's and grandmother's getting together and praying. Many of them are Pastors now.

We sent out seven churches when we were in New Mexico. We sent one church into Mexico City, four into Colorado, one in Houston, TX and one in Raton, NM. God did a powerful work in Las Vegas, New Mexico.

The time came when God wanted us to leave and pioneer again. Fred always wanted to pioneer in San Francisco. I didn't want to go to San Francisco. I could've stayed in New Mexico forever. I was content with my life. A mother of two; a thriving church and I had built strong relationships with the ladies there. I wanted to stay in New Mexico and continue building the church. However, Fred felt called to preach in San Francisco. So, during the Annual Church Conference in June 1993, he spoke to Pastor Warner.

When Pastor Warner said "wait," I took that to mean that it wasn't going to happen. So, I continued on with my life in New Mexico. I was doing what God called me to do – being busy.

Four years later, Pastor Warner said "yes." At this point, I wasn't ready. I was deeply involved in the church in New Mexico – I didn't want to leave.

Nevertheless, I felt God saying that He had shook the covers, "make your bed and move on." Such is the life of a pioneer Pastor. No sooner do you build relationships and root yourself in a place that you have to uproot and leave again. Mentally and emotionally, I wasn't ready to go. I just had to surrender my will, trust God and trust what my husband was hearing. I said "yes" to God's ways and God gave me peace about moving. It wasn't easy at all. I felt like I had to leave eleven years of my life behind. I had built relationships in New Mexico. Leaving New Mexico was a struggle.

In the midst of my struggle, God reminded me that I should have been praying about this four years ago. I hadn't been praying because I didn't think it was going to happen. Well, in some ways it was just easier to believe that it wasn't going to happen. So, when it did, I was unprepared and I just had to follow. We handed over the church in July 1997. We stayed with my mother-in-law in Tucson for a few months before moving to San Francisco.

Sunny San Francisco

We moved to San Francisco in September 1997; we pioneered in San Francisco for seven years. This was where I experienced the greatest challenges of my ministry. My kids became teenagers. Also, when I got to San Francisco, I realised I had to work.
God opened a door.

I managed to get a job working as a Receptionist at a Software Company. I worked there for four years. This was a challenging time for the economy, in particular many software companies were going bankrupt because of the Y2K, also known as the 'Millennium bug.' A lot of software companies couldn't transition from the year 1999 to 2000; a lot of the data was being lost and companies lost money. The company I was working for was very new, it had only been around for five years. They couldn't survive the Year 2000 bug. A lot of information crashed and they lost clients.

Months before the company started going under, my daughter got into a car accident so I had to quit my job to look after her until she got back on her feet. Six months after I quit the company went completely bankrupt. So, I couldn't go back. This was a difficult time because we were pioneering and doing many things for ourselves financially.

Eventually, my daughter got much better. In August 2002 she left San Francisco to attend University in Arizona. Whilst she was there, she gave her life to Jesus. Such a huge weight was lifted off of my shoulders. After my daughter left San Francisco, I had to find employment again. This was difficult because many people were out of jobs during this time but God is faithful.

Radisson Hotel

In October 2003, I got a call back from a hotel called the Radisson hotel. I was praying and believing God because I had never worked at a hotel, this was something very new. I also needed favour so that I could fit my job around the church schedule because hotels open 24 hours. I knew I wouldn't be able to work on a 24-hour schedule due to all of my ministry commitments. I just began to pray and trust God.

When I got to the hotel, I met with the General Manager; she interviewed me herself. Her name was Tiffany. This was unusual because the job I applied for was to work at the front desk, usually the Front Desk Manager would conduct these interviews. The General Manager is usually travelling and fulfilling other commitments, as the Radisson is part of a chain of hotels. Tiffany happened to be in town during the time of my interview and she said that she wanted to do the interview herself. I knew that it was God answering my prayers. One reason I know it was God is because when you get hired at a place like a hotel, you never get Sundays off. That was one of the things that I requested during my interview, the only way I could work there was that I had to have Sundays off. I knew that none of the other managers would've granted that request because there were so many other people that were there before me. I believe that God orchestrated this meeting. I had such peace.

I let Tiffany know from the outset that I was a Pastor's wife and that we were in San Francisco to pioneer a church. I explained to her the schedule of the church and also what 'invasion teams' meant. That was a terminology that she didn't understand, but as I began to explain it to her, she got it. God helped me through that interview. He put this Scripture in my heart and I held onto it.

"I can do all things through Christ who strengthens me."
Philippians 4:13

God gave me amazing favour because the General Manager offered me a job at the Front Desk on the spot; she was willing to work around my schedule with the church. I was able to work full-time and fulfil my commitments to ministry. None of the other managers would have had the authority to hire me and grant me all of those requests on the spot, so God led me straight to the person that could. God is faithful.

Overwhelmed with this immense favour, I wasn't sure how I was going to balance working and my ministry but God took control. I worked for a year at the Radisson between 2003 - 2004. During that year I was awarded the employee of the year award. There was such a grace that God gave me, the plaque was placed on the wall and that was a real testimony to the goodness of God. God is faithful.

When Pastors came in to preach for us, we would put them up at the Radisson Hotel and they would see the plaque and I would just say "God is good." I knew that it was totally God. God got me the job, He gave me His promise and He gave me favour. God was glorified. God used that hotel and that job so that we could afford to put Pastors who would come and preach for us into the rooms. This was a brand-new hotel; a Radisson and we were paying about $50 a night (about 1/3 of the price).

Looking back, I realise that God placed me in that job for a time such as this.

We were pioneering, we had pastors, we had revivals and they needed a place to stay. These Pastors were so blessed to be able to stay in such a luxurious hotel and the church was able to afford it because I was an employee and I got an employee discount. All around I can see that God knew exactly the timing of everything. God used the closing down of the Software Company to show me that it was time to move on. God put me in that job at the Radisson Hotel for the church; that job saved the church a lot of money.

During this time, I was also able to start a women's prayer group in my house; it became a place for us women to draw close together. The church grew slowly but God gave us precious people. After seven years of being in San Francisco, our core was 40 people strong and most are still serving God until this day.

Prescott, Arizona
In August 2004, Fred and I got a call from Pastor Wayman Mitchell to come on staff as the Assistant Pastor in Prescott.

In October 2004, we moved to Prescott Arizona. I was happy to move to Prescott, I wanted to learn. When we got there, we just served and tried to be a blessing to Pastor Mitchell and Sister Mitchell. I began to help out in all of the ministries that were there. I also wanted to get to know Sister Mitchell, she was a great woman of God, with so much wisdom. I remember her being in her 70's and still serving in the nursery. I was astonished.

Furthermore, seeing the longevity of her faithfulness and humility gave me a glimpse of what God can do with the life of somebody who is willing to just serve. Prescott was a place of refuge; it was a time of refreshing from the busyness of pioneering. It was also a time of learning.

At the Prescott Conference in January 2006, Fred and I were announced as Evangelists.

Tucson, Arizona
A few weeks later, by February 2006, my husband and I left Prescott and went back to Tucson to Evangelise. Being back in the Tucson church was such a strange experience for me because we left there in 1986 - that was twenty years ago. I was completely lost for words at this point, being back in Tucson didn't make any sense to me at all. I felt like we were in a waiting room. I had two choices, thrive or survive.

Fred was receiving calls from all over the world to go and preach. I didn't go with Fred when he went to preach. I tried to at first but I just got too tired to travel. Instead, I stayed in Tucson and I started helping to run the nursery and other ministries there.

After about nine months of Evangelism, Pastor Warner asked Fred to come on staff. So, in November 2006 (no conference), Fred became Pastor Warner's Associate Pastor. Once again God had given us an opportunity to serve and learn just as we did in Prescott, Arizona. We stayed in Tucson for eleven years in total.

One of my ministry highlights was joining the women's bible study, another one was helping to co-ordinate our annual church conference. We had much more responsibility in Tucson than we did when we were assisting in Prescott. I remember there were six months when Pastor Warner was not in church and we had to function as the Pastors on the ground reporting back to Pastor Warner as he nursed a severe wound from home. I got comfortable being back in Tucson. I thought this was it. My son was with us; I was re-united with my daughter and I was a grandmother.

"God, you want me to leave everything behind?"
In June 2017, Fred and I were out to lunch and we got a call from Pastor Warner. He said that he wanted us to go and take over the mother church in South London, England. This time was different from all of the others, this time I wasn't ready to go.

I could understand San Francisco because I always knew that Fred wanted to pioneer there. I had finally gotten used to being back in Tucson, but I had never been to England.

This time was more than just a case of surrendering my will and following my husband. I was a grandmother now, I had three grandsons, Kevin, Jayden and Jacob. My mother was eighty years old. In my mind I started listing off all of the reasons as to why I could not do this.

I found myself saying "I can't do this." For the first time in my life, I found myself saying "no" to God. I told myself that I was doing the right thing; I was a grandmother; my grandsons needed me. I asked God to give me an affirmation that this was really what He wanted for us. I never asked for affirmation like this before; this time was different. The burden on me was heavy because I was thinking about my grandsons. One of my grandsons, Kevin, has special needs. He was eight years old at the time and I knew that he needed me to help him. God told me that Kevin was going to be ok. But I still wrestled. I couldn't bring myself to give up my responsibilities as a grandmother.

Later on that day, I was at church setting up in the nursery about an hour before the service. Fred was awaiting my answer about London. He needed to give Pastor Warner our decision before the service started. I still didn't know how to process it. When Fred approached me, I said "no" to him because I couldn't bring myself to say "yes." He gave Pastor Warner our decision straight away.

Standing in the worship service, I looked to the side and I could see Fred's countenance. I knew that he was disappointed by my decision. Also, I felt such a heaviness in my heart that I couldn't lift my hands during the worship service. I tried to reason with God. I tried to convince myself that I was doing the right thing but God didn't lift the burden. I couldn't worship because I knew that God was not pleased with my decision. After I stopped wrestling with God, I turned to Fred during the worship and I said "yes." Immediately I changed my mind and the heavy burden was lifted. I felt that God was pleased with my answer, it was like God was smiling at me. Fred went to the backstage area and gave Pastor Warner our answer that we would do it. I had a real peace about it. I was able to worship and enjoy the service.

Parting the Red Sea

During our church conference in June 2017, Fred I and were announced to go and take over the church in South London. We had a timetable because Fred wanted us to be in London before the October 2017 conference. God re-affirmed that this was what he wanted because He started opening doors in preparation for us to go to London. I saw God move in ways that humanely getting these things done would've taken so much more time. We arrived in London at the end of September 2017 –a few days before the Conference. What God did for us in just one month was another affirmation that this was what He wanted. God opened doors that man could not open. It only took us 30 days to get approval to enter the country for the initial six months; this was a miracle because it usually takes months or even years to get that approval.

Another affirmation came when God processed my grandson Jayden's paperwork to travel abroad with us. I'm his Guardian, both his parents are in the military. At this time, his father was in a warzone in Syria and his mother was in Germany. Immigration Officials were asking for parental signatures – it seemed like an impossible situation. This lawyer that God put in our path sorted everything out by the Grace of God. We were able to get Jayden's paperwork sorted before we left in September. My daughter dropped him to us a couple of months later in November 2017. This was God parting the Red Sea for me.

During the time that we were preparing to move to London there was a sister in the church that gave me a Word. She said that she was praying for me and she didn't know what this meant, but God just told her to share it with me anyway:

"Your experience going to London Norma is going to be like this sweater that doesn't fit you right away, it's like I'm seeing you put this sweater on and you're trying to kind of fit into it. As you're fitting into it, you're kind of struggling' there's going to be the challenge of fitting into this sweater. But eventually this is a sweater that you are going to grow into. Maybe God has already put it in your heart that this is going to make sense to you when you get to London."

It was a very unique word; I normally don't get many words. However, this lady has a testimony of being a prayer warrior. I knew that she had been praying for me and seeking God for me and I believe that God gave her that Word to share. I put that in my mind and kept it in my heart. When I came to London it was like remembering that God had parted the Red Sea for me, especially emotionally. There was this peace that God had given me and I didn't question it.

I never really prepared myself to leave Tucson. I thought that I was going to fulfil my destiny there, by being a grandmother. When God said that He needed me in

London, He affirmed to me in many ways that it was what He wanted.

For such a Time as this:
Being here in London I'm realising, by how God has used me, that it really was accredited, "For such a time as this." I have seen God open doors and use our lives for His Glory. Coming to London I saw the church; the amazing responsibility; the conferences. The church is so vibrant and we have been able to work with both couples and young people. We have been blessed being a part of something like this.

We spent eleven years in Tucson, we got to work with a lot of couples and young people. We were also able to help coordinate a conference of a couple thousand people. Coming here wasn't overwhelming because God gave me such a confidence. I went to school for this. God took me and He put me in His own school for such a time as this. Everything that God has done up until this point – getting me the job in the Hotel; giving me favour – these things are visible to me. They have shown me that I can do all things through Christ who strengthens me.

We have been in London for over three years now. I have since received news that my Grandson Kevin, is doing really well and is learning how to ride a bike. God has kept His promises to me. The exciting thing about being here is seeing what else God has for our lives. I think about that Scripture in 1 Corinthians 2.

But as it is written: "Eye has not seen, nor ear heard, Nor have entered into the heart of man

The things which God has prepared for those who love Him."
1 Corinthians 2:9

This has always been God. I don't know how it's going to end but I know that it is going to be good. His plans are always to further the kingdom of God. I have learnt to say, "God if you give me the confidence then I will say yes, surrendering."

London is a place of realisation. I saw it for the first time but it became familiar. The sweater started to fit. I don't need to be overwhelmed here because God is the same. The same God that helped me in San Francisco and Tucson is the same God that is with me in London. He is the Author and the Finisher of my faith. I haven't arrived. The exciting thing about being in London is seeing what God has done and is doing in His church and the fact that we get to be a part of it.

The sacrifice will never compare to the blessing of having a surrendered heart and being obedient because what we have to sacrifice is nothing compared to what God has already sacrificed for us. My trophies are people; those who have come to know Jesus and seeing lives changed. I'm excited to see what God is going to do here. When you are in God's school, you are always going to learn if your heart is surrendered. There are some things you may not understand until you take the next step, but my anchor is surrendering to Him. God will close doors that are not right for this time and open doors that He knows it's the right season for. This is a plan that we didn't force because God gave us favour. The things that we were able to get done in a month of preparing to move here would have been impossible without God.

In relation to the word that that sister gave me back in Tucson, I haven't completely fitted into the sweater yet but I am a work in progress. I pray that I continue to fit into that which God has given me. My heart is to serve God's people and I'm excited to see what God has for us. One thing I know is that the South London church needs its own building. My prayer is, God do for the South London Church what you did in Las Vegas, New Mexico.

Being here is a miracle because I never expected to be abroad in such an amazing church. This is something that we have not earned, it's something that others have laboured in but we just pray that we are able to do our best to take it to wherever God wants us to take it for His glory."

Message to My Maidservants:
There are many times in life when God can send you to places and you can say, "For such a time as this." God has a plan and a purpose for our lives. He orders and directs our steps from place to place and season to season in order to bring us to an expected end.

For I know the thoughts that I think toward you, saith the LORD, thoughts of peace, and not of evil, to give you an expected end.
Jeremiah 29:11 KJV

That expected end is called Destiny. We all have a destiny in God – things that God pre-determined for us to do. However, God has also given us free will. Our destiny in God doesn't change, but it is possible that we may not reach it if we choose to disobey God and not walk in our calling. God wants us to walk in our calling.

After reading this book, you may not have reached your final destination yet, but you have to be sure that where you are right now, is the place that God wants you to be.

Woman of Destiny. You were called into the kingdom for such a time as this.

Message #12 For such a time as this

Reflection & Prayer

✧ ✾ ✧

Message to My Maidservants

Message #12 For such a time as this

Message to My Maidservants

About the Author

Desiri Okobia is an author, playwright, and creative educator whose work explores themes of faith, identity, and spiritual growth. Through her storytelling, she encourages readers to listen for God's voice and walk confidently in the calling placed on their lives.

She is the author of several books, including *Kitsu's Diary: The Things I Wish I Knew When I Was Fifteen*, which was nominated for the 2021 Author Elite Award for literary excellence, and *Message to My Maidservants: From His Mouth to Our Ears*, a devotional for women who desire to grow deeper in their relationship with God and serve Him faithfully in every season of life. Her other books include *Diaries of a Visionary: Inspiring Dreams* and *I Am Bodel*.

Alongside her writing, Desiri creates original stage productions and screen projects that explore identity, purpose, and transformation. She wrote, directed, and performed the role of Mrs Cleopatra in the stage production *Meet the Kids*, a thought-provoking play exploring the lives and challenges of young people growing up in London.

Her stories continue to develop across literature, stage, and screen as she explores new ways to bring meaningful narratives to life. She lives in London, UK.

Connect with Desiri online for updates on future books, theatre productions, and speaking engagements.

Message to My Maidservants

www.ingramcontent.com/pod-product-compliance
Lightning Source LLC
Chambersburg PA
CBHW072012070526
44583CB00015B/1445